A COMPREHENSIVE GUIDE TO EXCHANGE-TRADED FUNDS (ETFs)

To Mark

Joanne M. Hill, Dave Nadig, and Matt Hougan

With an appendix on international ETFs by Deborah Fuhr

CFA Institute
Research
Foundation

Statement of Purpose

The CFA Institute Research Foundation is a not-for-profit organization established to promote the development and dissemination of relevant research for investment practitioners worldwide.

Editorial Staff

Elizabeth Collins
Editor

Cindy Maisannes
Manager, Publications Production

Pat Light
Assistant Editor

Mike Dean
Publishing Technology Specialist

Biographies

Joanne Hill currently serves as head of Institutional Investment Strategy at ProShares, a premier provider of alternative exchange-traded funds (ETFs) with more than $25 billion in assets. Her responsibilities include portfolio strategy, product research, and education. Prior to joining ProShares in 2009, she spent 17 years at Goldman Sachs, where she was a managing director leading global equity index, quantitative, and derivatives research. A recognized leader in the financial industry, Dr. Hill was recently named 1 of the 10 inaugural recipients of the Top Women in Asset Management Awards by *Money Management Executive*. Dr. Hill is a recipient of the William F. Sharpe Indexing Lifetime Achievement Award and has published extensively. She is co-president of Women in ETFs and was one of its five founding members. Dr. Hill has served on the editorial boards of the *Financial Analysts Journal* and *Journal of Portfolio Management*. She is on the board of the "Q" Group and heads the Research Committee. She is also on the investment board of the Montgomery County Schools Pension System. Earlier in her career, she was an associate professor of finance at the University of Massachusetts (Amherst). She received a PhD in finance and an MBA from Syracuse University.

Dave Nadig is vice president and director of exchange-traded funds at FactSet Research Systems, where he spearheads the in-depth ETF and asset class research of the FactSet ETF Team. Mr. Nadig has been involved in researching, reporting on, and analyzing the investment management industry for more than 20 years. As the chief investment officer of ETF.com, the leading independent authority on exchange-traded funds, he built the world's most authoritative ETF data and analytics business (sold to FactSet in 2015). As a managing director at Barclays Global Investors, he helped design and market some of the first exchange-traded funds. With partner Don Lufkin, he went on to found MetaMarkets.com, a revolutionary transparent mutual fund company that pushed fund disclosure to the top of the US SEC agenda. As co-founder of Cerulli Associates in the early 1990s, he conducted some of the earliest research on fee-only financial advisers and the rise of indexing. Mr. Nadig is widely quoted in the financial press, is a regular speaker at finance conferences, and publishes a widely read blog at ETF.com. He has an MBA in finance from Boston University.

Matt Hougan is president of ETF.com, where he runs the company's US business and heads up its editorial efforts globally. Mr. Hougan is widely quoted in the media and is a frequent guest on CNBC. He is a regular contributor to the *Wall Street Journal*'s "The Experts" series on wealth management and a featured ETF columnist for the *Journal of Financial Planning*, *Financial Advisor* magazine, and CNBC.com. A three-time member of *Barron's* ETF Roundtable, he was named 1 of the 25 most influential people in the ETF industry by ETF Database and was one of Registered Rep's "Ten to Watch in 2012." Mr. Hougan graduated from Bowdoin College with a degree in philosophy.

Deborah Fuhr is managing partner and co-founder of ETFGI, an independent research and consultancy firm that offers paid-for research subscription services on trends in the global exchange-traded fund and exchange-traded product industry, the institutional users, and its ecosystem. Previously, she served as global head of ETF research and implementation strategy and as a managing director at BlackRock/BGI. Ms. Fuhr also worked as a managing director and head of the investment strategy team at Morgan Stanley in London and as an associate at Greenwich Associates. She received the 2014 William F. Sharpe Lifetime Achievement Award for outstanding and lasting contributions to the field of index investing. Ms. Fuhr is one of the founders of Women in ETFs. She is on the editorial boards of the *Journal of Indexes* (United States), *Journal of Indexes* (Europe), and *Money Management Executive*; the advisory board for the *Journal of Index Investing*; and the investment panels of experts for *Portfolio Adviser*, the FTSE ICB Advisory Committee, the NASDAQ listing and hearing review council, the International Advisory Committee for the Egyptian Exchange, and the University of Connecticut School of Business International Advisory Board. She received her bachelor's degree from the University of Connecticut and her MBA from the Kellogg School of Management at Northwestern University.

Acknowledgments

The authors wish to extend a special thanks to research analyst Stacey Brorup, ETF.com, for invaluable assistance in the production and editorial work associated with this book. Leigh Chikos contributed editorial assistance on many of the chapters. We are also grateful to Laurence B. Siegel, director of research at the CFA Institute Research Foundation, for his idea for the project several years ago and improvements to the manuscript with his insights, questions, and editorial expertise. Finally, we would like to acknowledge CFA Institute Research Foundation Executive Director Bud Haslett for guiding the project through its long path and providing critical support along the way.

Contents

Foreword

Timing is everything—in investment markets and in life. And although this book may seem in many ways long overdue, the timing of its publication is, in truth, perfect. The massively positive disruption of the exchange-traded fund (ETF) revolution, which began in the 1990s, is actually just now achieving full stride.

I am pleased to be writing the foreword to this book, especially because all three authors are friends and long-time colleagues. I have known and worked with Joanne Hill—including editing each other's book chapters—since 1997 and worked with Dave Nadig and Matt Hougan for more than 10 years each. They are all thought leaders in the ETF industry and are recognized for their ability to clearly communicate complex financial ideas to both general and professional audiences. Thus, they are the ideal authors for this book.

ETFs, in their 25-year history, have become one of the fastest-growing segments of the investment management business. These funds provide liquid access to virtually every asset class and allow both large and small investors to build institutional-caliber portfolios. The foundation for the growth of ETFs was the secular growth of indexing, which began 20 years before the first ETFs were launched in Canada (1990) and the United States (1993). Indexing is at the heart of a process that has moved the investment industry from art to science, and the growing popularity of index-based investment has forced all asset managers and advisers to improve their precision and value proposition.

The growth of ETFs (and indexing more broadly) and the expansion of their use is what makes this book's publication so timely—and so important for CFA candidates and charterholders to fully absorb. Although the structure of the ETF vehicle was recognized by financial experts as a superior package as early as the 1990s, now it is being appreciated by an ever-growing group of investors, product developers, investment firms, and asset owners.

It is important to recognize that the growth of the ETF industry was built on the foundations of the arguably even more important field of indexing—the application of efficient market theory and quantitative science to portfolio construction. The full list of pioneers who nurtured the concept of indexing is a long one, and I have been privileged to work with many of them as well as at two of the successor firms that first launched index funds.[1]

---

[1]The complete historical roots of indexing are summarized in Binu George, Steven Schoenfeld, and Jim Wiandt, "The Foundations of Indexing," Chapter 2 in *Active Index Investing: Maximizing Portfolio Performance and Minimizing Risk through Global Index Strategies*, edited by Steven Schoenfeld (New York: Wiley Finance, 2004).

Two outstanding contributors are Burton Malkiel and John Bogle. Malkiel brought to the public the idea of market efficiency and the superiority of broadly diversified index funds for long-term investors. Bogle then applied this logic to the practical world of investing by launching, in 1975, the first index mutual fund, thus opening up indexing to individual investors. The validation and recognition of indexing was cemented when William Sharpe made a clear case that the average actively managed dollar has to produce a performance equal to the average indexed dollar after costs and fees.[2] These and many other pioneers of indexing laid the foundation of both theory and practice for the launch and explosive growth of ETFs. Active managers in virtually every asset class are now evaluated relative to benchmark indexes after fees and have struggled to consistently outperform.[3]

"The Revolution Has Just Begun"

I felt confident writing the phrase "The Revolution Has Just Begun" more than 11 years ago in *Active Index Investing* as I described the growth of both indexing as a whole and ETFs.

Back then, all indexed assets (including massive institutional portfolios) were estimated to comprise 10%–11% of worldwide assets, and barely $150 billion was invested in ETFs.[4] Skeptics posited that neither area would grow much more; my prediction that ETFs would grow to more than $1 trillion in assets was considered wildly overly optimistic. Yet, these innovative financial vehicles have become one of the most important forces shaping how investors invest and how the market itself functions.

Now, in early 2015, more than 1,600 ETFs are listed in the United States, with approximately $2 trillion in total assets. Indexed assets across all investment strategies and vehicles account for more than $20 trillion. Just as one can now use an ETF vehicle with an index-based strategy for virtually every asset class, ETFs are now the preferred vehicle for factor-based strategies (formerly known as "enhanced indexing") and will be preferred soon for many actively managed strategies. The outlook for continued growth is strong. In each of the past five years (ending with 2014), ETFs attracted more than $100 billion in net inflows, swamping the inflows to traditional—and mostly

---

[2]William F. Sharpe, "The Arithmetic of Active Management," *Financial Analysts Journal*, vol. 47, no. 1 (January/February 1991): 7–9.
[3]For a recent summary of active manager performance relative to benchmarks, see "SPIVA® U.S. Scorecard Year-End 2014," S&P Dow Jones Indices Research, McGraw-Hill Financial (March 2015): www.spindices.com/documents/spiva/spiva-us-year-end-2014.pdf.
[4]Steven A. Schoenfeld, "The Revolution Has Just Begun!," Chapter 31 in *Active Index Investing*, op cit.

actively managed—mutual funds. ETFs now represent more than 12% of all fund assets in the United States, up from less than 2% in mid-2000. ETFs usually represent between one-quarter and one-third of US exchange volume.

To understand this growth—and continued potential—one needs to understand the fundamentals of ETFs, which is what this book so comprehensively delivers. It covers the full story of the evolution of ETFs as products and how they are used in investment strategies. It details how ETFs work, their unique investment and trading features, their regulatory structure, how they are used in tactical and strategic portfolio management in a broad range of asset classes, and how to evaluate them individually. The authors concisely explain the following broad advantages that ETFs provide compared with earlier investment vehicles:

- *Access.* ETFs are a true democratization of investment access and capabilities. With them, an individual investor can construct sophisticated global strategic allocations in all asset classes in way that was previously available only to large institutional investors, such as pension funds. Furthermore, ETFs make available to all investors even areas that were barely accessible to institutional investors, such as frontier markets and emerging market local currency bonds. Finally, individuals and their advisers can construct tactical allocation strategies that incorporate a wide range of approaches that combine disparate asset classes and sub-asset-class slices based on style, size, and sector.

- *Transparency.* For investors, ETFs provide a huge leap forward in transparency. Investors know what is in their portfolios, and even the naming of funds is greatly simplified.

- *Liquidity and Price Discovery.* Price discovery is especially vital for the smaller, less-liquid segments of US equities, foreign markets (especially when they are closed), and many corners of the fixed-income market. For foreign stock markets, especially during times of financial crisis, even knowing the right price can be challenging. Since the late 1990s, country ETFs have played a vital role in providing both liquidity and price discovery. The first example—and, in some ways, still the best example—is Malaysia during the 1997–98 Asian financial crisis, when capital controls were imposed on foreign investors. Institutions were "locked into" Malaysian stocks; repatriation was complex and at times impossible. The US-traded Malaysia WEBS ETF (now known as iShares MSCI Malaysia) was the only freely trading investment vehicle for this market. It was used by virtually the entire US investment community (custodians, asset managers, asset owners, and even some index providers) to value Malaysian equity holdings.

Similarly, during the global financial crisis of 2007–2009, which featured wild volatility in both equity and debt markets, ETFs were often the most reliable price signals, especially for certain types of fixed-income securities. The price discovery role of ETFs has continued to this day; both Russian and Greek equities often found an equilibrium price in the US ETF market during 2014 and early 2015.

- *Tax Efficiency and Fairness.* ETFs have revolutionized the efficiency and equity of tax treatment for investors. ETFs generally are able to provide in-kind redemptions by delivering a basket of securities and thus rarely need to make capital gains distributions. This feature allows most ETFs to avoid taxable events that arise from selling securities for cash within the fund. Not all ETFs are so tax efficient, but as the authors point out, ". . . overall, the record is exceptional." About 50% of all equity mutual funds paid out capital gains in 2013, whereas fewer than 5% of ETFs did, and rarely did ETFs pay gains that were significant.

ETFs for Every Asset Class and Investment Strategy

The authors' review of various asset classes that ETFs have opened up for all investors is comprehensive and highlights how the ETF vehicle has changed access for investors. The overview and taxonomy of each major category of ETFs alone make the book of value to investors. Equity ETFs, fixed-income ETFs, commodity and commodity equity ETFs, currency ETFs, alternative ETFs, and leveraged and inverse ETFs are explained together with a discussion of the increased prevalence of *combined* strategies, such as currency-hedged equity ETFs and commodity stock ETFs. Moreover, the authors cover the brave new world of factor tilt, alternatively weighted, and smart beta indexing and ETFs. Some confusion still afflicts the industry about "smart beta" and how closely it is based on enhanced indexing and earlier versions of alternatively weighted indexes. Smart beta is, in many ways, enhanced indexing but is now baked into index construction and design.

Finally, the book provides a discussion of asset allocation with ETFs and the growth of "ETF strategists" who use index-based strategies in actively managed portfolios. I call this approach "active indexing." With ETFs, investors and their advisers can be as active as they want to be. The area of ETF managed portfolios is also a revolution that is just getting started. The efficiency of the ETF vehicle is empowering and facilitating disruptive competition to traditional financial advisers through the growing "robo-adviser" business models—notably, Wealthfront and Betterment. Recently, the entry of Schwab Intelligent Portfolios has deepened this field. These new investment services could not exist if not for the liquidity, transparency, and ultra-low cost of index-based ETFs.

I congratulate the CFA Institute Research Foundation for publishing this vital book. And I warmly congratulate the authors, who worked long and hard, for writing it. I am sure that current and future generations of CFA candidates and charterholders and other sophisticated investors will greatly benefit from this book. And finally, congratulations to the reader for picking up the book—and, hopefully, reading it in its entirety. The ETF revolution has just begun, and the reader will gain from the book a great sense of the foundation that has already been built.

New York, April 2015

Steven A. Schoenfeld
Founder and Chief Investment Officer
BlueStar Global Investors, LLC

Part I
ETF Background, Features, and Analysis

1. Introduction: Why the Growth in Exchange-Traded Funds?

The purpose of this book is to help investors understand and use exchange-traded funds (ETFs).[5] Introduced just some 25 years ago, ETFs are now one of the fastest-growing segments of the investment management business. This book covers the details of how ETFs work, their unique investment and trading features, and how they fit into portfolio management. It also covers how best to evaluate ETFs to identify the right funds to fit any particular investment or trading objective.

Exchange-traded funds provide liquid access to virtually every corner of the financial markets, allowing investors big and small to build institutional-caliber portfolios with management fees significantly lower than those typical of mutual funds. High levels of transparency for both holdings and the investment strategy help investors easily evaluate an ETF's potential returns and risks.

At their core, ETFs are hybrid investment products, with many of the investment features of mutual funds married to the trading features of common stocks. Like a mutual fund, an investor buys shares in an ETF to own a proportional interest in the pooled assets. Like mutual funds, ETFs are generally managed by an investment adviser for a fee and regulated under the Investment Company Act of 1940. But unlike mutual funds, ETF shares are traded in continuous markets on global stock exchanges, can be bought and sold through brokerage accounts, and have continuous pricing and liquidity throughout the trading day. Thus, they can be margined, lent, shorted, or subjected to any other strategy used by sophisticated equity investors.

Although some other kinds of mutual funds—traditional closed-end funds, in particular—also trade on an exchange, today's ETFs are different. They typically disclose their holdings at the start of every trading day, so potential buyers and sellers can evaluate the traded ETF price versus the price of the underlying holdings. Specialized traders can create and redeem shares at the end of the day for net asset value, a feature that helps keep ETF market prices aligned with "fair value."

As of the end of Q1 2014, there were 1,570 ETFs listed in the United States, with a total of almost $1.74 trillion in assets under management. In

---

[5]Throughout this book, we use "ETF" as a generic acronym for a range of exchange-traded products, including those organized under the Investment Company Act of 1940, various trust structures, and exchange-traded notes.

2013, ETFs represented more than 11% of all mutual fund assets, up from 2% a decade earlier, and they continue to attract both individual and institutional investor assets. Even more impressive, on any given day, ETFs typically represent between 25% and 40% of the total dollar volume traded on US exchanges.

In short, in 20 years, these innovative financial products have gone from an afterthought to one of the most important forces shaping how investors invest and how the market itself functions. The outlook for continued growth is strong. For the four years ending 2013, ETFs attracted, respectively, $188 billion, $188 billion, $119 billion, and $122 billion in net inflows. At the end of Q3 2013, almost 1,000 new ETFs were registered at the US SEC. Recently, such mutual fund giants as PIMCO have moved aggressively into the ETF space and other firms, including Fidelity, T. Rowe Price, and Janus, have filed papers with the SEC to do the same. Experts ranging from BlackRock to McKinsey & Company expect overall assets to double in short order. In Chapter 14, we address the future of ETFs in detail in terms of investor applications and product development.

Benefits of Using ETFs as Investment Vehicles

An analysis of the ETF market must start with the central question: What are the features of ETFs that have made these funds so successful?

Costs and Benefits of Index Strategies.
Ask most investors why they own ETFs, and the first answer they will give is lower cost. The average mutual fund investing in US equities had an expense ratio of 1.37% in 2013, whereas the average US equity ETF expense ratio was 0.45%. ETFs now routinely offer exposure to broad areas of the markets at extraordinarily low costs: As of Q1 2014, an investor could gain exposure to a broad cross section of US equities for as little as 0.04% per year; emerging market equities cost as little as 0.14%.

The cost savings come, first and foremost, from the fact that most ETFs are index funds and, therefore, do not bear the costs of discretionary, active portfolio management. But index ETFs tend to be cheaper even than indexed mutual funds for investors operating at the retail level. (The story is mixed for institutional investors or those with separately managed accounts of significant size.)

Why the savings?

The primary reason for ETFs' cost advantage is implied by their name: The funds are *exchange traded*. When you buy or sell an ETF as an individual investor, you do so through a broker on an exchange. The costs of recording who you are, sending you prospectus documents, handling inquiries, and other factors are all borne by the broker. From the ETF manager's point of view, it only has a handful of "customers"—the brokerage firms where client accounts are kept.

By contrast, in the mutual fund world, individual investors can interact directly with the fund company. Distribution and recordkeeping costs, therefore, accrue to the fund, raising the overall cost of ownership. These generalities have some wrinkles, but the overarching message is borne out by the data: ETFs are generally cheaper to run than traditional mutual funds, active institutional strategies, and certainly hedge funds. Thus, ETFs are generally cheaper to own.

Access. A second core benefit of ETFs is simply access. ETFs have created a wealth of new portfolio construction opportunities for a broad range of investors by opening up new asset classes for investing. Prior to the growth of ETFs, owning such assets as gold bullion, emerging market bonds, currencies, volatility, or alternative assets was difficult and costly except for large institutional investors. ETFs have made all areas of the capital markets accessible for any investor with a brokerage account.

That last point is key. Because of their exchange-traded nature, ETFs offer a level playing field, providing all investors, regardless of the size of their investment holdings or time horizon, access to a full suite of products across the financial marketplace. In addition, ETFs can be sold short and, in some cases, have inverse exposure as an investment objective; this feature makes access possible for those seeking to profit from decreases as well as increases in price.

Transparency. The traditional asset management industry does not place a high value on transparency, which can harm investors in various ways. By law, mutual funds are required to disclose their portfolios only on a quarterly basis—and even then, only with a lag of up to 60 days. Hedge funds and institutional fund managers tend to report performance and positions four times a year, a few weeks after quarter-end. Between these reporting periods, investors generally have no idea whether a fund is invested according to its stated investment objective or the manager has taken unexpected risks. Funds can and do stray from their described targets—a phenomenon known as "style drift"—which can negatively affect an investor's asset allocation plan.

Lack of transparency also creates the opportunity for hidden exposure problems. If an active mutual fund decides between reporting periods to take a significant position in a particular security, this action leaves an investor who is holding that security separately "doubled up." Institutional managers can stray from their set tracking errors relative to their benchmarks, and hedge funds can vary their leverage, gross and net exposures, and positions.

Most ETF providers, in contrast, display their entire portfolios on a daily basis through their websites, and this information is also picked up by financial data services. (An exception—as of the end of Q1 2014—is Vanguard, which only reports full holdings on a monthly basis.) This transparency can be enormously helpful in portfolio construction and analysis. *Actively managed* ETFs must by law disclose their full portfolios every day, making them the most transparent of all ETFs (and indeed of all fund products).

Finally, most ETFs use relatively clear names based on the indexes they track—for example, iShares Russell 2000, Vanguard Total Bond Market, ProShares Inverse S&P 500—whereas some of the most popular mutual funds have somewhat generic names—Fidelity Magellan, PIMCO Total Return, Growth Fund of America. Although there are, of course, exceptions, clarity is the rule with ETF names.

Liquidity and Price Discovery. The fourth major benefit of ETFs is their liquidity. Being exchange traded, ETFs can be bought or sold on secondary markets at various times throughout the day. They can be held on margin, shorted, optioned, and so forth. Anything you can do with a single stock, you can do with an ETF.

Therefore, ETF users include many more investors than those who would buy mutual funds; from hedge funds to institutional investors to traders, users of ETFs are diverse. Because they trade like equities, these fund products have democratized the investment process, providing a marketplace where all types of investors, regardless of asset size or length of time horizon, can come together and transact in a transparent manner with the regulatory protections of exchange-traded stocks and, in most cases, registered investment companies.

ETFs are not, of course, the only exchange-traded fund vehicles. Long before ETFs were popular, investors regularly bought and sold shares of closed-end funds on the open market. The distinguishing feature of ETFs— and what makes them so successful—is that, unlike closed-end funds, they have a mechanism that improves their ability to trade close to their true net asset value (NAV) throughout the day.

Specifically, ETFs have an open and extended creation/redemption mechanism that allows market participants to create or redeem shares of an ETF at the end of each day at fair value. The creation/redemption mechanism is covered in detail in Chapter 3, but in short, it allows investors to arbitrage between the ETF itself and the underlying securities that compose it. If the price of an ETF gets out of line with the fund's value, market makers will typically jump in to bring prices back in line.

This aspect is obviously good for investors because it ensures that they get a fair price for their sales. But it is also good for another reason: It facilitates the price discovery process for ETFs. This process is well developed and relies on financial intermediaries regularly comparing ETFs with the vehicles' underlying securities and with related products. In fact, ETFs are an important product for broker/dealers, who have trading desks competing for customer order flow and looking for arbitrage opportunities between ETFs and other products, such as portfolio trades, swaps, options, and futures on similar indexes. These desks are structured to commit capital, provide information on the ETFs, and answer execution questions for institutional investors, registered investment advisers, and their financial adviser networks.

For many illiquid or poorly priced markets, ETFs are becoming a serious source of price discovery. When the municipal bond markets became extraordinarily illiquid in the fall of 2010, for instance, the ETFs tracking municipal bonds became the only source of liquidity in that market. They provided a way for investors to buy or sell those bonds at a time when the primary markets were effectively frozen. Indeed, many now think that ETFs provide the most accurate pricing of fixed-income portfolios and indexes in the market.

Similarly, when the Egyptian stock markets closed in the Arab Spring of 2011, ETFs tracking the Egyptian market continued to trade and provide a window into market expectations for the region. Such situations are quite volatile, of course, but by providing liquidity in those unusual circumstances—or in such markets as fixed income, where price discovery is weak as a rule—ETFs serve a vital function.

Tax Efficiency and Tax Fairness. Another key benefit of ETFs to investors is tax efficiency. In most situations, ETFs have a marked advantage over mutual funds when it comes to after-tax returns. There are two reasons for greater tax efficiency with ETFs: lower portfolio turnover and the ability to do in-kind redemptions. Index strategies that serve as the basis for most ETFs and some mutual funds tend to have lower turnover than actively managed strategies; thus, they do not expose investors to capital gains distributions as large as those generated by the typical actively managed mutual fund.

Capital gains distributions are the dirty little secret of the mutual fund industry. Each year, hundreds of mutual funds pay out capital gains distributions to shareholders for a variety of reasons. For example, they must sell an appreciated stock to generate cash for withdrawals or for portfolio rebalancing, or they may hold a stock that is acquired by another firm. At the end of the year, the active funds distribute these gains to shareholders, who must then pay taxes on them.

In contrast, ETFs that have the ability to do in-kind redemptions rarely need to make any kind of capital gains distribution. Redemptions often are handled by delivering a basket of securities rather than cash. This ability allows most ETFs to avoid taxable events that arise from selling securities for cash within the fund. In 2013, for instance, the largest ETF provider, iShares, paid out capital gains on only 4 of its 299 ETFs, and those payouts were generally small. Not all ETFs are so tax efficient. Bond ETFs, commodity ETFs, and leveraged and inverse ETFs, for example, have paid out large capital gains distributions in the past, as have funds invested in the less-liquid or more-active strategies. But, overall, the record is exceptional: In 2013, according to the Investment Company Institute, fully 51% of all equity mutual fund share classes paid out capital gains. Only 3.87% of ETFs did. And of that 3.87%, a tiny fraction—only seven funds—paid out gains that were significant (more than 2% of NAV).

This deferral of tax until an investor actually sells a position can make a substantial difference in returns. An investor in the SSgA (State Street Global Advisors) S&P 500 Index mutual fund (SVSPX), which made regular capital gains distributions, had a compound annual after-tax return of 6.77% in the 10 years ending 30 November 2011. According to Morningstar, an investor in the SPDT S&P 500 ETF (SPY) would instead have avoided paying capital gains taxes along the way and would have paid taxes only on final sale of the shares, thereby earning an after-tax return of 7.12%. That is a difference of 35 bps a year, mostly the result of the tax advantage.

ETFs also provide an excellent opportunity for tax loss harvesting. Normally, if an investor wants to sell a security to book a loss, the "wash sale rule" prohibits the investor from claiming it if a "substantially identical" security is purchased within 30 days. This rule can cause problems for a long-term asset allocation strategy. With an ETF, however, investors can often sell one fund and replace it with another tracking a different but similar index and thus maintain the exposure while capturing the loss.

Caveats

ETFs have numerous benefits, but investors should be aware of a number of potential drawbacks before using them in an investment strategy.

New Asset Classes = New Risks. Investors new to ETFs and their sometimes-novel asset classes and strategies may be unfamiliar with the underlying assets, drivers of return, and associated risks. Even an investor who is well versed in the international equity market may not be familiar with the inherent risks of, say, international corporate bonds, direct currency investing, or emerging market small-capitalization stocks. Those exposures have not been offered in a mutual fund package with any regularity, but they are significant and regular features of the ETF landscape.

Furthermore, many alternative ETFs—funds providing exposure through futures, notes, or swaps—involve portfolio structures, counterparty risks, and unfamiliar tax treatment, not because of the nature of the underlying exposures but because of the means of accessing them. ETFs offering exposure to commodities, leveraged and inverse returns, currency, or volatility are particularly subject to this caution. Investors considering the less conventional investment strategies may need to dive deeper into the features of the strategies than they would when investing with stocks and bonds, which are more straightforward investments. Education is the key to understanding the various risks in certain asset classes and strategies.

Transaction Costs. Although ETFs have lower expense ratios than mutual funds, some costs must be considered that could differ from those associated with mutual funds. With exchange tradability comes the burden of paying commissions, bid–ask spreads, and, potentially, premiums and discounts to NAV. As with trading stocks, these costs can affect returns. In the case of an institutional mutual fund, the fund incurs the costs of buying and selling the underlying securities with each day's cash flow or changes in portfolio holdings. The trading costs of commissions and market impact show up in fund performance but are otherwise largely hidden from the mutual fund investor.

Recently, a growing number of "commission-free" trading programs for ETFs have reduced trading costs for certain investors, but even within commission-free programs, ETF investors must still pay spreads. These costs are real and, for some investors, prohibitive.

Using ETFs in 401(k)s: The Next Frontier. The retirement market has been a tremendous source of assets for the traditional mutual fund industry, largely through defined-contribution plans, such as 401(k) and 403(b) plans. Indeed, the vast majority of defined-contribution assets in the United States makes use of mutual funds. The recordkeeping systems for these programs rely on the fact that individuals can purchase fractional shares of a mutual fund—something that can be difficult with an exchange-traded product. Although the recordkeeping industry has developed some workarounds, ETFs are currently a troublesome fit for investors in defined-contribution plans, most of whom do not have brokerage services for exchange access. Moreover, some of the key benefits of ETFs—tradability and tax efficiency—are largely irrelevant to many 401(k) investors.

ETFs as a Disruptive Invention

In summary, it is fair to say that ETFs have changed the face of investing. With lower fees, greater transparency, expanded access, and greater tax efficiency than traditional mutual funds, they are attracting assets from those funds and threatening classic fund distribution models. With ETFs' inherent liquidity, they are also altering the trading landscape by providing a market where hedge funds, pension funds, and other institutional investors can connect their order flow with that of high-net-worth and other individual investors and can engage in price discovery for illiquid assets.

ETFs have also made top-down and cross-market investing more accessible by providing tools that can be used in asset or sector allocation, factor-tilt strategies, and thematic investing. They have helped many investors incorporate dynamic strategies in their portfolio management processes by allowing them to adapt to shifting return and risk opportunities.

Broadly, ETFs are encouraging a new approach to investing that focuses on macroeconomic and thematic developments rather than single-stock investing. ETFs encourage investors to consider that the choice between China and India is more important than the choice between Intel and AMD, that diversifying into oil futures or emerging market bonds is more helpful than adding yet another active equity manager to a portfolio. And as a product without a load-based commission structure, ETFs are also accelerating the transition to fee-based fiduciary adviser–investor relationships.

These characteristics represent a fundamental shift in the way the financial community operates. In a world where one-third of all trading volume takes place in ETFs, does the value of macroeconomic research rise and the value of single-stock research fall? In a world where hedge fund replication strategies exist that charge less than 1% a year, can the 2-and-20 model stay intact for non-top-tier hedge funds? In a world dominated by macro trends, should traditional active stock pickers feel threatened?

Over the past few years, instances of backlash against ETFs and their role in the marketplace have occurred. People have accused them of corrupting the price discovery mechanism of the stock market, of posing a systemic risk to finance, and of steering investors into inappropriate and complex investments. Congressional hearings have been held; SEC and U.S. Commodity Futures Trading Commission studies have been conducted; and the financial media have extensively explored the influence ETFs have on market structure and market operations.

In the end, the harshest parts of these criticisms do not hold water. But they do highlight that whenever a new and disruptive technology comes along, significant and in-depth education is needed.

ETFs are powerful tools that require lower costs, expand strategic choices, and provide ease of access with transparency. When investors use ETFs appropriately, they can improve their return–risk profiles. Like any powerful tool, however, ETFs can be dangerous if not properly understood.

2.   From Mutual Funds and Tradable Indexes to ETFs: The Landscape

To fully understand ETFs, an investor can benefit from understanding where they came from. In this chapter, we briefly discuss the history of mutual funds and the rise of indexing. From that point, we can cover the history of ETFs. We examine the ETF landscape by asset class and identify the largest ETFs as of the end of Q1 2014.

Mutual Funds and the Rise of Indexing

Investors have long looked for ways to expand their investment horizons. Historians note that pooled investing vehicles first appeared sometime near the turn of the 19th century in Europe. The first closed-end fund in the United States was the Boston Personal Property Trust, which began in 1893, although similar funds were common in Europe as early as the beginning of the 1800s. In 1924, the modern mutual fund was born in Boston with the creation of the first open-end fund, the Massachusetts Investors' Trust. The fund went public in 1928; it still exists today.

Before the stock market crashed in October 1929, a number of open-end mutual funds and an even larger number of closed-end funds were competing for investors' dollars. After the crash, most of these funds were wiped out, although some small open-end funds managed to survive. The industry started to grow in the 1930s with the aid of two key pieces of legislation emerging from the Great Depression—the Securities Act of 1933 and the Investment Company Act of 1940. (We discuss these acts in detail in Chapter 3.)

With the creation of mutual funds, investors were able to pool money with like-minded individuals and have professionals manage the investments. Investors thus gained the benefits of diversification and economies of scale in fund trading, recordkeeping, and performance measurement and reporting. The first mutual funds created in the 1940s under the new federal regulations were actively managed investment vehicles with individual stocks picked by experts who were trying to get the highest returns possible. Sometimes they were right, and sometimes they were wrong—a situation that persists to this day.

The Rise of Indexing. In the 1970s, modern portfolio theory (first introduced by Harry Markowitz in the 1950s and enriched by William Sharpe and others in the 1960s) began to be incorporated into institutional investment products. Together with these innovations came the concept that investors might be better off "buying the market" than picking individual stocks. This idea was popularized by Burton Malkiel in his seminal 1973 book *A Random Walk Down Wall Street*. Institutions gradually began following that advice, and large institutional asset pools, such as pension plans and endowment funds, began investing in private portfolios that mimicked the popular S&P 500 Index.

The first index fund was a strategy structured by Wells Fargo Investment Advisors for the Samsonite Corporation pension fund in 1971. The first index mutual fund, launched by John Bogle of the Vanguard Group, became available in 1975. Since that time, US equity index funds as a percentage of US mutual fund assets have grown tremendously. As shown in **Figure 2.1**, their share of total mutual fund assets has grown since 1998 from less than 10% to the point at which they now represent close to 20% of all mutual fund assets.

Most ETFs are, in their investment processes and organization, simply an extension of index-based mutual funds. They are a new delivery vehicle that happens to be more tax efficient, have lower cost than index funds, and be available on an exchange. Increasingly, however, they have been dominating the battle for flows and stealing market share from both active and index-based mutual funds. In addition, they have helped fuel the expansion in the range of choices available in an index fund format to specialized equity

Figure 2.1. Equity Index Mutual Funds' Share of Overall Assets, 1998–2013

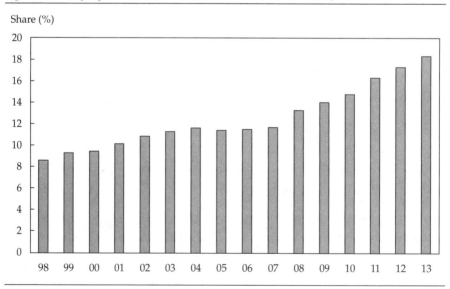

Source: Investment Company Institute 2014 Factbook.

©2015 The CFA Institute Research Foundation

and fixed-income categories, as well as to commodities and even rules-based investment strategies.

Mutual Fund Basics. Mutual funds were initially the only way an investor could participate in an index product, and they remain a primary tool for accessing index-based investments today. Because they are familiar to many investors, mutual funds provide a good place to start explaining how ETFs work.

Imagine that a US investor wants $10,000 in S&P 500 exposure through a mutual fund. The investor places a buy order in one of two ways—either directly through the fund company or indirectly via a brokerage account. Regardless of the approach, at the end of the day, the order is to buy $10,000 of the mutual fund at whatever the "fair" price is.

Importantly, whether the investor places the order at 10:00 a.m., 2:00 p.m., or 4:00 p.m. eastern standard time does not matter: The trade is executed only at the end of the day, after the close of trading, at the fund's net asset value.

The NAV is calculated once a day for all mutual funds. To determine the NAV, all of the investments in a given mutual fund are added together and valued on the basis of closing prices (or some measure of fair value for international investments). Then, the total portfolio value is divided by the number of shares the fund has issued. The end result is the NAV per share.

That per-share NAV price determines exactly how many shares of the fund $10,000 will buy. If the NAV is $125, the investor will own 80 shares of the mutual fund. The mutual fund company is responsible for sending out all paperwork associated with the fund to the shareholders and must keep track of who the investors are and how many shares they own. Typically, the fund has staff on hand to answer questions. All of these business expenses are paid for by the fund's investors through fees charged by the fund company.

After the investor's order has been processed—something that takes place after the close of trading in New York—more work remains. The next morning, the fund has the investor's $10,000 sitting in cash on its books. Unless the fund wants to maintain a cash position, it must put that money to work in the market. Trading costs and price slippage in allocating that capital are both part of the deal.

Now, follow the path forward. Suppose the mutual fund manager (and the S&P 500) performs exceptionally well and the value of the fund doubles. The investor's 80 shares are now worth $20,000 ($250 per share). When the investor decides to sell, the process reverses itself. The investor places an order to sell the shares. At the end of the day, the fund company sends the investor a check for the value of the holdings (based on the NAV). The next day, the manager goes into the market to sell enough securities to cover the check.

This daily batched processing has a lot of advantages. First, because the shares in the fund are notional units, investors can come and go at any time. New shares are created when new money comes in; old shares are deleted from the books when money goes out; and everyone trades exactly at NAV. The obvious challenges are the lack of intraday pricing and the costs associated with both the paperwork and the allocation of new capital. These challenges are what the ETF structure addresses.

Origins of an Innovation: How the Crash of 1987 and the Technology Bubble Gave Birth to the ETF Industry

ETFs trace their roots back to the concept of "program trading," a computer-based innovation in the 1980s that allowed investors to purchase or sell all the shares of a major index (such as the S&P 500) through a single trade order defined as the list of index stock tickers and shares in each. Over the years, a number of attempts were made to package these trades into a single product, but none truly caught on until the early 1990s with the launch of the first ETF.

Along Came a Spider. Many consider the S&P 500 SPDR (Standard & Poor's Depositary Receipt), with the ticker SPY, to be the oldest ETF, but it was not actually the first: That honor goes to the Toronto Index Participation Shares, which launched on the Toronto Stock Exchange in 1990; it offered exposure to 35 of the largest companies in Canada. Despite some initial success, however, that ETF never truly caught on and was shut down.

SPY was the first ETF launched in the United States and remains the oldest—and most successful—ETF in the world. The idea for SPY was born at the American Stock Exchange in the early 1990s. Working with a variety of partners—including State Street Global Advisors (SSgA)—Nathan Most and Steven Bloom of the Amex created a structure that pioneered many of the key features of every ETF on the market today: SPY offered exchange-traded access to a major market index and relied on an ongoing creation/redemption mechanism to keep the ETF's market price tracking closely to fair value throughout the day. SPY ended its first year with $475 million in assets under management (AUM) and today is the largest ETF in the world.

Product Expansion and the Launch of a Giant. The ETF industry did not sit idle for long. In 1995, the second ETF was added to the market, when SSgA introduced the S&P 400 MidCap ETF under the ticker symbol MDY. But ETFs remained isolated products at that point.

The ETF "industry" began to take off in 1996 when Morgan Stanley launched WEBS (World Equity Benchmark Shares) and hired Barclays Global Investors to manage the ETFs. These products provided exposure to a variety of individual country indexes from Morgan Stanley Capital International (MSCI). These products were revolutionary in three ways.

First, they marked the entrance of institutional indexing giant Barclays Global Investors (BGI) into the ETF investment universe. BGI would later negotiate a deal with Morgan Stanley to take control of the WEBS ETFs and rebrand them as iShares. BGI would then go on to be the undisputed leader in terms of ETF assets on a global basis.

Second, in contrast to SPY and MDY—which were both unit investment trusts—WEBS were organized as mutual funds under the Investment Company Act of 1940.[6] This structure was more familiar (and friendly) to end investors and became the structure under which most future equity and bond ETFs were managed.

Third, WEBS revealed the power of ETFs to offer price discovery in various markets. Although WEBS sometimes tracked markets that were closed during the US trading day, investors could still act on their opinions about in what direction those markets *would have been* trading had they been open. For instance, before WEBS, a US investor with an opinion on Japan had to wait until the Japanese markets opened to act on that opinion; with WEBS, he or she could trade on that opinion at any time. For this reason, the products found tremendous traction among both institutions and traders.

Qs and iShares Shift ETFs into Mainstream Financial Products. Despite the success of WEBS and the original SPDRs, ETF trading was still a relatively small corner of the financial markets for most of the 1990s. As of 1998, total industry assets were only $15.6 billion.

In 1999, two key new participants broadened the product's appeal. In the age of extraordinary interest in technology stocks, the NASDAQ 100 Index, dominated by the largest technology stocks trading on the NASDAQ Stock Market and followed by many investors, was the bellwether index. The Bank of New York created a trust based on the NASDAQ 100 Index (NDX) and launched it as an ETF called "QQQ" or "Qs" (the NASDAQ 100 Index Tracking Stock). The response was overwhelming: From a dead start, QQQ attracted $18.6 billion in assets in its first year of trading. Moreover, it became the go-to tool for hedge funds, mutual funds, and others looking to tactically trade, hedge, or gain exposure to technology stock holdings. During a time

---

[6]The various structures are detailed in Chapter 4.

when being out of the market for a week could mean missing an 8% move, the ability to equitize cash—intraday—was tremendously well received.

Meanwhile, BGI, under the leadership of Patricia Dunn, was getting serious about the ETF business. A team led by Larry Tint—as well as Lee Kranefuss, a consultant to BGI at the time—convinced Dunn that by focusing on the marketing and distribution framework already so successful with mutual funds, BGI could compete for the assets flowing into this industry by introducing a wide range of index products via ETFs. BGI was already a market leader in institutional index fund management. It had funds across a broad spectrum of benchmarks—Standard & Poor's, Russell, and MSCI. The firm used this position to negotiate contracts with these index vendors and, in 2000, launched more than 50 ETFs under the iShares label.

These ETFs included the original WEBS (renamed) and additional products providing a variety of exposures to US equities. By offering a wide portfolio of ETFs, iShares opened up new possibilities: Investors could now create *portfolios of ETFs*, rather than using single products to equitize cash. BGI also created a substantial and sustained education effort to teach financial advisers about the merits of ETFs and index-based investing, and the penetration of ETFs into the retail channel began. The firm also fielded an ETF sales force, who marketed ETFs in a manner similar to mutual funds. This helped financial advisers evaluate the investment (rather than just trading) features of ETFs.

Vanguard, PowerShares, and Other Entrants. Vanguard, the leader in index mutual funds, began thinking about this new distribution channel as a way to capitalize on its already strong position in index mutual funds. Despite some objections from founder Bogle—who publicly criticized ETFs as too short term a trading vehicle—Vanguard innovated by devising a legal structure that issued ETFs as a special share class of its existing mutual funds. The Vanguard products, introduced in 2001, were called "VIPERs" (Vanguard Index Participation Equity Receipts).

The next firm to enter the market in a serious way was PowerShares, an independent firm that, in 2003, launched two ETFs tracking quant-based indexes aimed to outperform the market. These ETFs were the first designed specifically as buy-and-hold investments targeting the retail and financial advisory markets, and they had some success, attracting $1.14 billion in assets during the next three years.

With the slow recovery in the 2000s from the bursting of the technology bubble in the late 1990s, retail investors were largely turning away from equities and moving into fixed income and commodities. As a result, dreams of a large retail ETF user base were delayed. Throughout the middle part of the 2000s, hedge funds regularly accounted for 70%–80% of ETF trading activity and institutions dominated asset flows.

ETF companies continued to innovate, however, and they found new success in the commodity and fixed-income markets. The launch of SPDR Gold Shares (GLD) in 2006 was one of the most successful ETF launches of all time. GLD attracted more than $1 billion in assets in its first three days of trading. The year 2006 also saw the launch of the first oil ETFs, among other products. Also in 2006, ProShares gained SEC permission to launch leveraged and inverse ETFs (similar mutual funds had been available since 1993). The new funds relied on derivatives to provide both leverage and short exposure in a fund trading vehicle that had a daily objective based on a multiple of index performance. These products quickly grew to become a significant part of ETF trading, offering the tools of leverage and shorting to a broad range of investors.

Snapshot of the ETF Industry as It Moves into Adulthood

More than two decades have passed since Toronto's Index Participation Shares became an attractive way to access Canadian equity index exposure and the S&P SPY captured the interest of US investors. ETF assets now span a variety of asset classes and trading strategies. In **Table 2.1**, we show that US and international equity ETFs still make up the bulk (78%) of the $1.7 trillion in US ETF assets as of the end of Q1 2014, similar to the percentage at the end of 2009 after the financial crisis decimated equity returns. Fixed-income and commodity ETFs had grown to become, respectively, 12.5% and 9.7%. With assets growing in the past few years at a clip of well more than $100 billion a year, fixed-income ETFs have become a slightly bigger slice of the pie (15.2%), but commodities have shrunk to only 3.9% of the growing ETF assets.

The number of ETFs traded on US exchanges in early 2014 is close to 1,600, and the average expense ratio is 63 bps, or 0.63%. The highest-cost categories are those covering commodities, alternatives, and ETFs incorporating leveraged and inverse strategies. Of special note are the newer categories "asset allocation" and "alternatives," both of which are growing parts of the mutual fund industry. They have begun to see an increase in interest and product offerings in the ETF space also but have yet to build up significant assets.

Table 2.1. ETF Share of Overall Assets by Asset Class, 31 March 2014

Asset Class	AUM ($ billions)	% of Total AUM	# of Funds	Average Expense Ratio
US equity	945.1	54.43	422	0.46%
International equity	408.8	23.55	434	0.59
US fixed income	242.6	13.97	167	0.26
International fixed income	21.6	1.25	61	0.53
Commodities	67.1	3.86	116	0.86
Currency	1.9	0.11	24	0.52
Leveraged	21.5	1.24	125	1.03
Inverse	20.4	1.17	140	0.99
Asset allocation	4.2	0.24	37	0.65
Alternatives	3.1	0.18	42	1.31
Total	1,736.2		1,568	0.63%

Note: Columns may not total because of rounding.
Source: ETF.com.

Table 2.2 and **Table 2.3** show the largest 20 ETFs by assets as of, respectively, 2010 and the end of Q1 2014. In 2010, the asset cutoff to make this list was $8.7 billion, but by the end of Q1 2014, the top 20 cutoff had almost doubled to $16.2 billion. First-mover advantage has always been key in the ETF industry, and the first US-based ETF, SPY (SPDR S&P 500), was the largest in assets in both periods. Its assets were slightly under $90 billion in 2010 versus $157 billion in 2014. Combining SPY assets with IVV (the iShares fund benchmarked to the S&P 500) and the VOO (the Vanguard S&P 500 ETF), more than $228 billion were invested in the S&P 500 through ETFs as of early 2014. Other large ETFs covering the total US stock market as well as small-cap and mid-cap indexes are found on the list in both periods (VTI, QQQ, IWM, and IJH). Two US sector ETFs are also now included in the largest ETFs list: the Vanguard REIT ETF, VNQ, and the Financial Select SPDR, XLF, with $21 billion and $18.7 billion, respectively.

International and emerging market equity ETFs are high on the list in both periods, showing that ETFs benefited from the push by US investors to expand their portfolios to take advantage of return opportunities and diversification abroad. At the end of 2010, EEM and VWO, both benchmarked to emerging market equity indexes, had combined assets of $92 billion; that figure had fallen almost 20%, however, as of Q1 2014. Table 2.3 shows that VWO, with $42.3 billion compared with $31.9 billion for EEM, moved to

Table 2.2. Largest ETFs by Assets, Year-End 2010

Ticker	Name	AUM ($ billions)	Asset Class
SPY	SPDR S&P 500	89.9	US equity
GLD	SPDR Gold	58.0	Commodities
EEM	iShares MSCI Emerging Markets	47.5	International equity
VWO	Vanguard Emerging Markets	44.4	International equity
EFA	iShares MSCI EAFE	36.8	International equity
IVV	iShares S&P 500	25.8	US equity
QQQ	PowerShares QQQ	22.1	US equity
TIP	iShares Barclays TIPS Bond	19.4	US fixed income
VTI	Vanguard Total Stock Market	18.2	US equity
IWM	iShares Russell 2000	17.5	US equity
LQD	iBoxx $ Investment Grade Corporate Bond	13.1	US fixed income
IWF	iShares Russell 1000 Growth	12.6	US equity
MDY	SPDR S&P MidCap 400	12.2	US equity
EWZ	iShares MSCI Brazil	11.7	International equity
AGG	iShares Core U.S. Aggregate Bond	11.2	US fixed income
SLV	iShares Silver	10.8	Commodities
IWD	iShares Russell 1000 Value	10.7	US equity
IJH	iShares S&P 400 MidCap	9.3	US equity
BND	Vanguard Total Bond Market	9.0	US fixed income
DIA	SPDR Dow Jones Industrial Average Trust	8.7	US equity

the lead in that competition. EFA has been the primary ETF used for accessing international developed markets. Its $37 billion of assets in 2010 grew to $54 billion in 2014, and it was joined on the top 20 list by the Vanguard FTSE Developed Market ETF, with $21 billion in assets.

The fixed-income ETFs with the largest assets are about evenly divided among several indexes. Some are broad indexes, such as BND (assets of $19 billion) and AGG (assets of $16 billion), and some are focused on corporate debt (e.g., LQD, with $17 billion in assets).

Filling out the list are a mixture of ETFs—metals, represented by GLD in both periods and SLV on the 2010 list; growth and value equity index ETFs; and a few funds representing sectors, countries, or thematic strategies. The rise of thematic investing through strategy indexes is demonstrated by the

Table 2.3.   Largest ETFs by Assets, End of Q1 2014

Ticker	Name	AUM ($ billions)	Asset Class
SPY	SPDR S&P 500	157.2	US equity
IVV	iShares Core S&P 500	54.4	US equity
EFA	iShares MSCI EAFE	54.0	International equity
QQQ	PowerShares QQQ	43.9	US equity
VWO	Vanguard FTSE Emerging Markets	42.4	International equity
VTI	Vanguard Total Stock Market	41.4	US equity
GLD	SPDR Gold	33.8	Commodities
EEM	iShares MSCI Emerging Markets	31.9	International equity
IWM	iShares Russell 2000	28.8	US equity
IWF	iShares Russell 1000 Growth	23.0	US equity
IWD	iShares Russell 1000 Value	21.3	US equity
VNQ	Vanguard REIT	21.0	US equity
VEA	Vanguard FTSE Developed Markets	20.8	International equity
IJH	iShares Core S&P Mid-Cap	20.6	US equity
BND	Vanguard Total Bond Market	19.4	US fixed income
VIG	Vanguard Dividend Appreciation	18.9	US equity
XLF	Financial Select SPDR	18.7	US equity
VOO	Vanguard S&P 500	16.7	US equity
LQD	iShares iBoxx $ Investment Grade Corp Bond	16.6	US fixed income
AGG	iShares Core U.S. Aggregate Bond	16.2	US fixed income

appearance of the Vanguard Dividend Appreciation ETF in the list of top 20 ETFs in Q1 2014. It is benchmarked to the NASDAQ Dividend Achievers Index, a set of stocks that have a record of increasing dividends over time.

The managers of ETF assets, ranked in **Table 2.4** by AUM, are another key part of the landscape. The largest three ETF sponsors—BlackRock, SSgA, and Vanguard—have a long history as leading index asset managers. (BlackRock purchased BGI in 2009.) Together, these three managers make up 80% of total assets and have the lowest expense ratios, consistent with the basic index exposures that make up their primary product line. Other major ETF providers, such as PowerShares, WisdomTree, ProShares, Van Eck, Guggenheim, and First Trust, represent about 13% of the industry and have positioned themselves primarily with offerings around strategy

Table 2.4. Largest ETF Sponsors, End of Q1 2014

Issuer	AUM ($ millions)	% of Total AUM	No. of Funds	Average Expense Ratio
BlackRock	673.2	38.77	296	0.40%
SSgA	379.6	21.86	130	0.37
Vanguard	351.2	20.23	67	0.14
Invesco PowerShares	99.9	5.76	161	0.60
WisdomTree	33.8	1.95	62	0.50
ProShares	27.4	1.58	145	0.97
Guggenheim	24.4	1.40	68	0.47
First Trust	23.9	1.38	85	0.71
Van Eck	23.4	1.35	62	0.67
Charles Schwab	19.0	1.10	21	0.16
PIMCO	14.6	0.84	21	0.38
ALPS	9.3	0.53	15	0.99
Barclays Capital	8.1	0.47	80	0.86
Northern Trust	7.6	0.44	15	0.40
Direxion	7.3	0.42	55	0.93
JPMorgan	5.9	0.34	1	0.85
UBS	4.4	0.25	31	0.76
Global X	3.4	0.20	40	0.72
ETF Securities	3.0	0.17	7	0.50
US Commodity Funds	2.0	0.11	12	1.35

indexes, thematic investing, and alternatives. Others on the list include some that specialize in exchange-traded notes (ETNs), such as Barclays Capital, JPMorgan, and UBS. (ETNs are not funds or pooled investment vehicles but are unsecured debt obligations of the issuer with a payout based on a stated index minus management fees.) ETF Securities and US Commodity Funds primarily offer commodity ETFs. Charles Schwab has focused on broad index ETFs at a low fee and with no commissions. PIMCO and Northern Trust are recent additions looking to build on their presence in mutual fund management and trust services.

In summary, the landscape of ETFs is lush with both traditional and new strategy-based index products and is gaining on mutual funds in terms of share of assets. In addition, ETFs are making major inroads into the portfolios of global institutional investors—from pension funds to hedge funds. Asset managers have been the slowest to expand use because they see themselves more as providers of products in this space. They intend to use ETFs in top-down and asset allocation fund products, however, especially where they can apply a discretionary or model-based portfolio management process.

In addition, the final pieces of the landscape are coming together in the form of conventional active strategies packaged into ETFs. These products are likely to be the means through which traditional mutual fund firms, such as Fidelity, T. Rowe Price, and Franklin Templeton, begin building their space. The breadth of product offerings and range of uses for various horizons and in various market conditions have set the stage for continued growth and innovation in ETF investment strategy applications. We discuss the uses of ETFs in portfolio management, in particular, in Chapter 7.

3.   The Nuts and Bolts: How ETFs Work

ETFs, by their very structure, work differently from the way mutual funds work. Those differences create the unique benefits ETFs offer—as well as some of their risks. In this chapter, we outline how ETFs work—from inception to day-to-day processing. Concepts covered are the creation/redemption process, fund seeding, and the roles of authorized participants, index providers and managers, brokers, and exchanges.

Creation and Redemption

ETFs are traded on stock exchanges like stocks. Unlike stocks, however, they do not get onto the exchange via an initial public offering. Rather, ETFs rely on a creation/redemption mechanism that allows for the continuous creation and destruction of ETF shares. Understanding how this mechanism works is the key to understanding both the benefits and potential risks of ETFs.

The Creation/Redemption Process. The process for creating and redeeming shares in an ETF is perhaps the most important and unique component of ETF functioning. The best way to understand the creation/redemption process is to picture it in action.

Imagine, as you did with mutual funds, that you want to put money to work in an ETF. The process is simple: You place a buy order in your brokerage account, and your broker arranges to buy those shares from another investor who wants to sell. The order is executed, and you receive shares of the ETF in your brokerage account just as if you transacted in a stock in the secondary market.

At this point, the ETF fund manager/sponsor is not involved in the transaction at all. The ETF firm does not know that you have bought these shares, nor does it receive any influx of money to invest. Shares simply transfer in the secondary market from one investor (the seller) to another (the buyer) and go through a securities exchange three-day settlement process.

The process sounds great, but if you can buy shares of an ETF only from another investor, where do the first shares come from? It seems like a chicken-and-egg problem.

The only investors who can create or redeem new shares of an ETF are a special group of institutional investors called "authorized participants" (APs). As the name suggests, APs are large broker/dealers, often market makers, that are authorized by the issuer to participate in the creation/redemption process. The AP creates new shares of an ETF by transacting with the ETF manager/

sponsor. In this sense, the AP interacts with ETF fund managers much like an individual investor interacts with a traditional mutual fund firm.

The AP, however, has a set of responsibilities and opportunities that go far beyond those of a typical mutual fund investor. When a mutual fund investor wants to buy new shares from a mutual fund firm, the investor simply sends that firm cash. Although certain ETFs (notably, certain bond ETFs) work this way, others operate by using what is called "in-kind" creations and redemptions.

Each day, an ETF manager publishes a list of securities that it wants to own in the fund. For instance, an S&P 500 ETF will typically want to own all the securities in the S&P 500 Index in the exact weights they appear in that index. The list of securities specific to each ETF and disclosed publicly each day is called the "creation basket." This basket also serves as the portfolio for determining the intrinsic net asset value of the ETF on the basis of prices during the trading day.

To create new shares, an AP goes out into the market and buys up all the stocks in the creation basket at the right percentages. The AP can also elect to use shares it holds, as a market maker, in its inventory. It then delivers this basket of securities to the ETF manager in exchange for an equal value in shares of the ETF. The AP can then go out into the market and sell the ETF shares to individual investors.

These transactions between the AP and the ETF manager occur in large blocks called "creation units," usually (but not always) equal to 50,000 shares of the ETF. The exchange is one for one—one carefully articulated basket of underlying securities in exchange for an equal basket of ETF shares.

The process also works in reverse: If the AP has a block of ETF shares to get rid of, the AP presents these shares for redemption to the ETF issuer and receives in return the basket of underlying securities, which the AP can then sell on the open market. This basket is often the same as the creation basket, but it may be different if the ETF is trying to get rid of a particular set of securities. The basket of securities the AP receives when it redeems shares is called the "redemption basket."

The actual process of exchanging baskets happens at the end of the day, but the AP can quote bid–offer spreads and execute trades throughout the day because the AP knows the composition of the basket that will be needed for deliverance or redemption at the end of the day. That necessary number is based on the AP's net long or short exposure after providing markets for the ETF that day. Because the creation basket is published each morning and is available to all market participants, an AP (or other market makers that have resources devoted to ETF arbitrage with the underlying basket) can sell

50,000 shares of an ETF at 10:00 a.m. in New York while simultaneously buying the basket of underlying securities because the AP knows its will be able to swap the basket for the 50,000 shares promised to investors during the course of the day.

This process is vital. The back-and-forth creation/redemption mechanism is key to keeping the price of an ETF in a tight range around the NAV of the portfolio of securities it holds. The factors that drive the width of the bid–ask spread and trading range around intraday NAV include the cost of arbitrage (buying the securities and selling the ETF) and such factors as volatility and liquidity (ongoing volume in the securities and the ETF). We discuss these factors in detail when we address ETF trading in Chapter 6.

Most investors, large and small, buy ETFs through their brokers, just as they do a stock. The price those investors pay is based entirely on supply and demand—as with a stock. If there are many more buyers than sellers, the price of the ETF goes up. If the price goes up more than the true value of the underlying securities would suggest is "fair," APs and other market makers that are set up to arbitrage ETFs become active in the market. Specifically, knowing they can buy the underlying securities and create new shares of the ETF at fair value at the end of the day, they start selling ETF shares at their inflated value.

The arbitrage gap—the price at which it makes sense for ETF market makers to step in—varies with the liquidity of the underlying securities and a variety of related costs; in some ETFs, the gap can be as small as 1 cent, whereas in other ETFs, it can be substantial. For any ETF, however, the gap creates a band around fair value inside which the ETF will trade. In other words, arbitrage keeps the ETF trading at or near fair value.

Let's take a look at how that works. In the scenario shown in **Figure 3.1**, the ETF is trading on the stock exchange at $25.10. The fair value of the ETF based on its underlying stocks, however, is only $25.00. So, an AP will step in and buy the basket of securities that the ETF tracks and exchange it

Figure 3.1. An ETF Share Price at a Premium to NAV

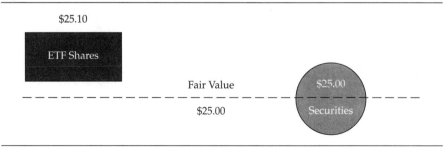

with the ETF provider for a creation unit. The AP will then sell those new ETF shares on the open market and pocket the $0.10 per share difference.

This action puts downward pressure on the price of the ETF (because the AP is pushing shares out into the market) and puts upward pressure on the prices of the underlying securities (because the AP went out into the market and bought the underlying shares). If the ETF share price continues to trade at a premium, the AP will repeat this process until no further arbitrage opportunity exists.

In the scenario shown in **Figure 3.2**, the price of the ETF is $24.90. The fair value of the underlying stocks is $25.00. Here, the AP market maker steps in and puts together a creation unit of ETF shares by purchasing them on the open market and redeems them with the ETF provider in exchange for the basket of the underlying stocks. The AP can then sell the stocks on the exchange and pocket the $0.10 per share price difference. Once again, if the share price continues to be at a discount, the AP will continue this process until no further arbitrage opportunity exists.

Of course, these scenarios are abstract and do not include the costs that the APs incur. The AP generally pays all trading costs associated with buying up the baskets and ETF shares and pays an additional fee to the ETF provider to cover processing fees associated with creation/redemption activities. If the AP is transacting at subcreation unit size—that is, if there is demand only for 30,000 shares—because the AP can create only in blocks of 50,000 shares, the AP must pay additional costs to hedge the remaining 20,000 shares until they can be rolled off the AP's books.

These and similar costs influence how large or small the premium or discount needs to be before the AP will step in with the creation/redemption process. Keep in mind that ETF desks at APs, as large and active financial market participants, are staffed with traders regularly making markets in ETFs and creating and redeeming. Hence, their commissions and trading costs are typically among the lowest of security market participants. They also

Figure 3.2. An ETF Share Price at a Discount to NAV

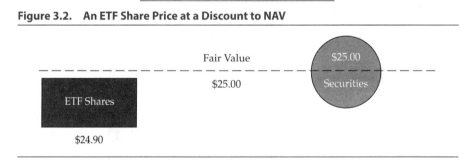

often consolidate ETF market making with other portfolio or index product trading activities, which helps keep their costs and net risks as low as possible.

A significant advantage of this system is that the AP absorbs all the costs of acquiring new securities for the fund. These costs are reflected in the spread, which investors pay only when entering and exiting the fund. Thus, existing and ongoing shareholders of an ETF are shielded from the negative impact of transaction costs from money entering and exiting a fund. In contrast, when a new investor enters a traditional mutual fund, any trading fees associated with putting that investor's investment dollars to work are borne by other shareholders in the fund. The same happens when an investor sells; the costs are spread among the investors who remain in the fund. By embedding the trading costs in the ETF spread, the ETF structure assigns the fee to the appropriate investors—the ones doing the actual buying and selling.

How Fair Value Is Assessed. As the price of the ETF moves during the day, investors would benefit from knowing whether the market price is a fair reflection of the price of all the fund's holdings. To track this information, ETF issuers are required by their exemptive relief from the SEC to contract with third parties to calculate and publish an intraday estimate of the value of an ETF share based on that day's holdings as disclosed in its creation basket.[7] This value is published every 15 seconds and is referred to as the "intraday indicative value," "intraday NAV" (INAV), or "indication of portfolio value"—all terms that mean the same thing.

Investors can monitor the INAV and the quoted price of an ETF to determine for themselves whether they are going to get a fair deal when buying or selling shares.

Caveat: Timing Differences. The scenario just described works perfectly for ETFs tracking US equities and certain other instruments for which the underlying holdings of the ETF trade during precisely the same hours as the ETF. Beyond US equities, however, investors need to be aware of both the difficulty an AP can face in managing creations and redemptions and the questionable utility of the reported INAV.

For example, imagine an ETF that holds nothing but stocks trading in Tokyo. During the course of the US trading day, none of those stocks can be traded. Thus, the reported INAV for the fund will be effectively flat (barring movements in currency). Investors will surely be trading the ETF shares on the basis of their perceptions of how the ETF's stock holdings *would be* performing, however, if the stocks were trading and how the stocks will open the next morning when the Tokyo exchange opens. The INAV is effectively

---

[7]Exemptive relief is discussed in Chapter 4.

"stuck," even as the ETF's share price engages in price discovery. In this situation, the INAV is no help in assessing fair value; in fact, it is misleading. Even in US non-equity securities these issues abound. **Figure 3.3** illustrates the issue of market hour overlap for ETFs in various asset classes.

APs, of course, have tools at their disposal to manage these timing discrepancies; futures and options on Japanese equity indexes, American Depositary Receipts, and proxy portfolios also trade in US hours, which helps APs estimate fair values when the underlying markets are closed. These hedges are not quite perfect, and the end results are also imperfect: Not only do spreads tend to be wider on ETFs trading outside of local market hours, but also, the assessment of fair pricing is far more of a judgment call than a science.

ETF Design for Success. The creation/redemption process is critical to ETFs working well, and the designer of an ETF has a tremendous ability to influence how well the process works for a fund. If the issuer demands that a creation basket be not 50,000 shares but 200,000 shares, the AP will have more difficulty stepping in to arbitrage when net new demand is lower than 200,000. Basket sizes may range from 10,000 shares for UBS Commodity ETNs to 600,000 shares for a handful of iShares ETFs. If the ETF holds highly illiquid securities, the issuer can alter the basket that APs must deliver, thereby lowering the costs of creation. In the most extreme case, the fund may allow for the creation of ETF shares for cash.

Issuers can also charge minimal or large fees for creation and redemption, which affects the AP's bottom line and thus the likelihood that the AP will step in to keep prices in line with fair value. Consider the fee of $50 for the Vanguard Short-Term Inflation Protected Securities ETF (VTIP) versus the fee of $28,000 for the Vanguard All-World Ex-US Small-Cap ETF (VSS).

Designers can also include or exclude "claw back" clauses for cash-based creations. Such clauses stipulate that the costs of putting that money to work can be charged back to the AP.

Trading and Settlement

Confusion abounds about how ETFs work. Claims have even appeared in the popular press that somehow ETFs are a special class of securities subject to different rules when it comes to the back-office processes. Although ETFs are truly unique, the reality is that from the perspective of an investor buying them on the open market, they go through the same settlement and clearing process as any other stock listed on the US stock markets. For the sake of clarity, this section elucidates that process.

Figure 3.3. Illustration of Market Hours Overlap

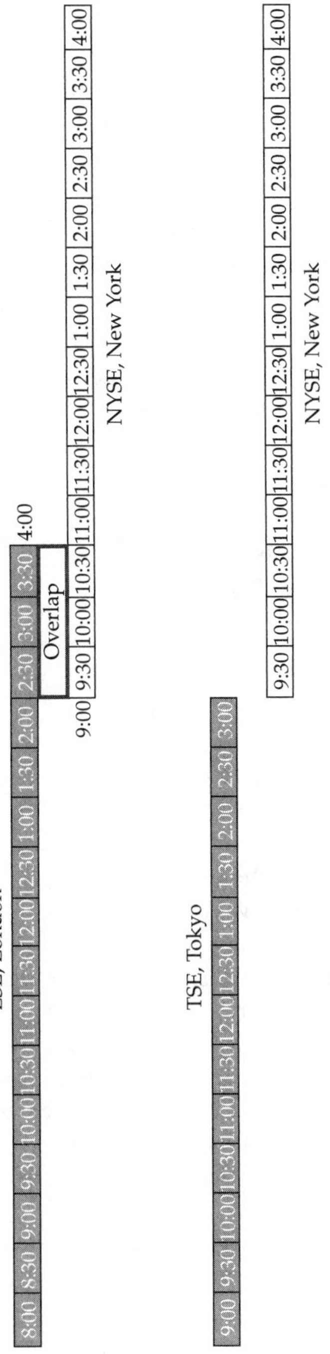

Note: LSE is the London Stock Exchange; TSE is the Tokyo Stock Exchange.

National Security Clearing Corporation and Depository Trust Company. All trades that have been made on a given day are submitted at the end of the day to the National Security Clearing Corporation (NSCC). The NSCC is responsible for matching up and clearing most trades through a nightly batch process. As long as both parties of a transaction agree that Party A sold Party B *X* shares of *Y* stock, the NSCC becomes the guarantor of that transaction on the evening of the trade and the trade is considered cleared. After this point, the buyer is guaranteed beneficial ownership in the stock (or ETF) as of the time the trade was marked "executed," even if something (e.g., bankruptcy) happens to the seller before the trade is settled.

The Depository Trust Company (DTC), of which the NSCC is a subsidiary, holds the book of accounts—the actual list of who owns what. This information is aggregated at the member-firm level, rather than at the individual-investor level. For instance, the DTC keeps track of how many shares of Microsoft are currently held by JPMorgan or Charles Schwab, but Charles Schwab is responsible for keeping track of which of its customers own which ETFs.

After each trade is cleared, the DTC then tallies up the total of all trades in a process of continuous net settlement. For example, suppose the following at the end of a trading day:

- E*Trade owes Schwab 500 shares of SPY.

- Schwab owes Bank of America Merrill Lynch 500 shares of stock SPY.

Then, from the DTC's perspective, Schwab is "whole": It both is owed and owes 500 shares of SPY. To settle the day's transactions, E*Trade's account will be debited the 500 shares of stock SPY and Bank of America Merrill Lynch will be credited 500 shares.

The NSCC has three days to complete this process and have each firm review its records and correct any discrepancies. This T + 3 settlement process works flawlessly for the vast majority of ETF transactions. The point at which people get confused concerns the market makers. Because the job of a market maker is to constantly buy and sell a given security, they are far more likely to end up genuinely short at the end of a given day. If, for example, a market maker sells securities to an investor at the close, the market maker's book may be unbalanced. It may show on the DTC books as short shares of a given name. For this reason, market makers are given up to six days to settle their accounts.

Often, a market maker can benefit from delaying settlement for as long as possible, especially for ETFs. For example, if a market maker/authorized participant is trading SPY, it might deliberately sell more SPY than it owns until it has sold enough to warrant creating a basket with the ETF issuer, thus making good on its sales. The longer the market maker delays basket creation, the longer it can avoid paying the creation fee (often $500–$1,000) and related execution costs. The delay also gives the AP more time before it has to take on responsibility for the full creation basket of ETF shares (often 50,000 shares).

ETFs with large expense ratios or embedded costs (such as the cost of maintaining swaps for leveraged/inverse ETFs) have a second incentive to delay settlement as long as possible. Although the market maker is short the ETF shares, the market maker is, in essence, "collecting" the fees and expenses of the position.

For investors, this timing issue is all largely academic because once the trade is made, the trade is guaranteed by the NSCC. Eventually, whether through market transactions or creation activity, all ETF trades do settle, just as stock transactions do.

ETF Shorting. One quirky result of the trading and settlement process is the dominance of ETFs on the shorted securities reports released biweekly by the SEC. For example, as of 31 March 2014, $157.62 billion was reported as short by investors through the short reporting system. Many investors worry when they see ETFs that have more shares sold short than seemingly exist. For example, SPDR Retail (XRT) had $720.51 million in assets under management as of the end of Q1 2014, but it had $2.06 billion in shares sold short.

This situation can happen in several ways.

First, because of the ETF creation/redemption system, more shares of an ETF can effectively be created "on demand." XRT tracks the retail sector of the S&P 500, a sector that is highly liquid and highly volatile, and the daily creation/redemption activity often results in widely variable assets under management. As shown in **Figure 3.4**, the actual number of shares outstanding of XRT varied from fewer than 3 million to more than 22 million over the three-year period ending Q1 2014. The number commonly fluctuates between 6 million and 18 million shares outstanding over only a few days.

Although a large number of shares of an ETF may be reported short, it does not necessarily mean the market contains "phantom" shares. The process for reporting shorts is notoriously buggy, and data frequently lag by days or weeks. Such a lag can serve to exaggerate inconsistencies.

Another situation that can occur is one of "cascading shorts." Imagine this scenario: An authorized participant wants to sell some shares to an institutional investor (Buyer 2). The AP does not actually own the shares, so the AP borrows them from a market maker (Buyer 1). The process works fine, and the ETF is now 100% short. From Buyer 2's perspective, however, it is the sole owner of the shares and can do whatever it wants with them. It decides to loan its shares to another institutional investor (Borrower 2), that then sells them short to Buyer 3, as shown in **Figure 3.5**. The ETF is now 200% short.

Figure 3.4.   XRT Shares Outstanding, 31 March 2011–31 March 2014

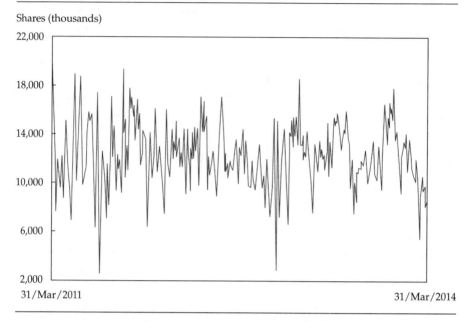

Figure 3.5.   Cascading Short Sales

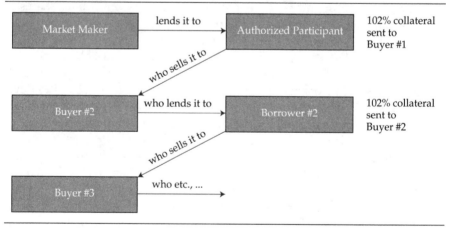

Nothing untoward has happened, and no real risk is embedded here. All the positions are overcollateralized, and the chain can quickly be unwound. If the original owner of the shares (the market maker) wants the shares back, the AP can simply create them (or recall them directly).

Note also in this example that only the retail investor at the end of the chain has an unencumbered claim on the shares. Everyone else in the chain knows they have lent out the shares, and if they want to redeem them, they need to recall and, most likely, new shares will need to be created.

The chain can produce frightening numbers—200% of an ETF's shares sold short—but the reality is not scary at all.

4. Regulatory Structure

After the stock market crash of 1929 and the subsequent Great Depression, faith in banks and investment firms hit an all-time low. To increase trust in these institutions and boost investment in the United States, the US Congress passed the Securities Act of 1933 and the Investment Company Act of 1940. These two pieces of legislation, commonly referred to as the 1933 Act and the 1940 Act—together with the Securities Exchange Act of 1934, which created the SEC—are the cornerstones of investment industry regulation.

ETFs actually exist as exemptions and loopholes to this existing legislation. To function, ETFs require exemptive relief from certain requirements of the 1940 Act and the 1934 Act.

The Base Case

The following subsections describe the relationship between ETFs and the 1933 Act and between ETFs and later regulatory legislation.

The 1933 Act and the Registration of Listed Securities. The Securities Act of 1933, also called the "Truth in Securities Act," provided for issuing shares on an exchange.[8] The 1933 Act outlines what information must be disclosed to allow investors to make informed decisions about investing in a company's securities. Information is required to be accurate, but the SEC does not guarantee its accuracy. Investors do have ways to pursue claims against a company, however, if the required information is found to be inaccurate.

The SEC states the two basic objectives of the 1933 Act as the following:

- to require that investors receive financial and other significant information concerning securities being offered for public sale and

- to prohibit deceit, misrepresentations, and other fraud in the sale of securities.

All ETFs (both those that are registered investment companies under the 1940 Act and those that are not) are subject to the Securities Act of 1933. It governs every equity-like vehicle available on public exchanges, and exchange-traded products of all kinds live under its umbrella.

---

[8]The full text of the 1933 Act is available at https://www.sec.gov/about/laws/sa33.pdf.

The 1934 Act (and Exemptive Relief from It). The 1934 Act governs how securities exchanges operate and establishes certain listing requirements. Without exemptive relief, several parts of how broker/dealers interact with ETFs would be problematic. The relief sought from the 1934 Act typically includes

- changes to how trade confirmations are communicated,

- changes to how corporate actions are communicated to end shareholders, and

- changes to how certain kinds of transactions among broker dealers are reported.

The 1940 Act (and Exemptive Relief from It). The Investment Company Act of 1940 regulates the organization of companies, including mutual funds, that engage primarily in investing and trading in securities.[9] The 1940 Act is designed to protect investors by minimizing conflicts of interest and requiring extensive disclosure of finances and investment policies. These disclosures are required at regular intervals on an ongoing basis and must include information about the fund, its investment objectives, and the investment firm's structure and operations. The 1940 Act also sets up restrictions on day-to-day operations. It does not, however, permit the SEC to directly supervise or pass judgment on the investment decisions made by the companies or funds. In other words, *caveat emptor*.

The 1940 Act established the concept of a registered investment company (RIC), which is similar to a corporation but has its own unique structure. Some examples of differences between RICs and corporations are the following:

- RICs have an independent board of trustees with fiduciary responsibility to run the RIC solely for the benefit of the investors.

- RICs can continuously offer and redeem shares.

- The tax structure of an RIC allows gains and losses to pass through.

The 1940 Act RIC is the basic structure of a US mutual fund, and the vast majority of ETFs in the United States are structured as 1940 Act RICs. To qualify under the 1940 Act, however, ETFs must receive exemptive relief from certain requirements. Receiving that relief is one of the first steps in taking an ETF to market.

---

[9]The full text of the 1940 Act is available at http://www.sec.gov/about/laws/ica40.pdf.

Typical exemptions that are requested include the following:

- The ability to trade individual shares of the ETF on a stock exchange at prices other than net asset value. Without this exemption, funds would be limited to trading at NAV directly with shareholders.

- The ability to redeem shares only in creation units rather than individual shares. Without this exemption, the AP function would not work.

- Exemption from the requirement to deliver a prospectus to every shareholder. Without this exemption, the recordkeeping required would be impossible because the issuer simply does not know who owns its shares.

Investment Company Act Release No. 17809 (1990). A final piece of legislation that contributed to the development of ETFs is the 1990 Investment Company Act Release No. 17809. This release grants exemptions from the 1940 Act and allows

> unit investment trusts to issue redeemable securities that are divisible into nonredeemable components, permits secondary market transactions in such redeemable securities at negotiated prices and approves the exchange of shares of an open-end management firm for units of beneficial interest in a unit trust.[10]

In other words, it paved the way for share creation and redemption throughout the day instead of only at the close of business—as is done with mutual funds—and allowed those shares to be traded on exchanges.

Alternative Structures

Although most ETFs are set up as RICs under the 1940 Act, exchange-traded, index-based, pooled vehicles are launched in other ways. When the 1940 Act provides a structure that is too restrictive for pursuing certain asset classes or strategies, ETF issuers use alternative structures. From the investor perspective, the alternative structures may appear similar to the common structure, which is why it is critical that investors examine a prospectus to assess the benefits, costs, and risks of the specific structure that is behind the ticker symbol of an ETF.

Trusts. The forms of trusts allowed by the legislation are unit investment trusts, grantor trusts, and commodity pools or trusts.

---

[10]See http://www.sec.gov/news/digest/1990/dig102290.pdf.

■ *Unit investment trusts.* Unit investment trusts (UITs) are allowed under the 1940 Act and regulated by it, but they differ in specific ways from RICs. Most importantly, UITs are more passive than ETFs structured as RICs. They cannot be actively managed or subject to human discretion; in fact, they do not have boards, corporate officers, or even an investment adviser.

This hands-off approach also means that no reinvestment of dividends received by the fund occurs. Instead, the dividends are held in a non-interest-bearing account until paid out. UITs also may not participate in securities lending.

The inability to reinvest dividends received can have a detrimental effect, called a "cash drag," on the tracking performance of the UIT. An example of the types will show how this drag works.

Both SPDR S&P 500 (SPY) and iShares S&P 500 Index Fund (IVV) track the S&P 500. Both are organized under the 1940 Act—IVV as an RIC and SPY as a UIT. IVV is able to reinvest any dividends it receives before paying them out quarterly to investors, and it usually does so by buying futures. SPY must hold all dividends in a non-interest-bearing escrow account until they are paid out quarterly. This difference leads to a slight performance disadvantage for SPY in up markets and a slight performance advantage in down markets. **Table 4.1** reports the performance for four periods ending in March 2014.

Note that Table 4.1 shows IVV outperforming SPY by a few basis points a year over a time period containing a bull market. In a down market, SPY would actually benefit from having the tiny cash position; SPY outperformed in the volatile five-year period from 1 April 2009 through 31 March 2014.

Structurally, a UIT must fully replicate the index it is tracking, rather than using any optimization or sampling method. This limitation is not a problem for broad indexes, but because security weightings are also restricted, replication can be a problem for industry sectors or country funds in which one or two companies make up a large portion of the index.

Table 4.1. Cash Drag on UIT Cumulative Total Returns, Periods Ending 31 March 2014 (in percent, compounded quarterly)

Period (years)	SPY (UIT form)	IVV (RIC form)
1	21.76	21.92
3	50.16	50.42
5	160.47	161.30
10	102.49	102.92

Finally, UITs have a termination date indicating when the product will be redeemed or canceled, although those dates can be decades out into the future. For example, the largest ETF structured as a UIT, SPY, according to its latest prospectus, has a termination date of 22 January 2118.

■ *Grantor trusts.* Grantor trusts may also be used in exchange-traded funds. Rather than being organized under the 1940 Act, grantor trusts are registered under the Securities Act of 1933. They hold a nonmanaged portfolio of assets that cannot be altered. If the portfolio contains securities, investors have voting rights on those underlying securities within the trust. Any dividends are distributed directly and immediately to shareholders of the trust.

Equity-focused grantor trusts once existed in the ETF structure, but by now, they have all been restructured as 1940 Act funds. Where grantor trusts remain significant are in the commodity market and, particularly, in funds representing ownership of physical bullion. The SPDR Gold Shares ETF (GLD), for instance, which aims to track the price of gold, is a grantor trust. GLD is not considered a commodity pool (discussed in the next subsection) and is not regulated by the Commodity Futures Trading Commission (CFTC) because the trust holds physical gold bullion, not futures. Shares are created and redeemed through the same AP creation/redemption process, only instead of securities, physical bullion and cash are exchanged for shares at NAV. For something as simple as GLD, the grantor trust structure works well and efficiently.

■ *Commodity pools/trusts.* Any futures-based ETF is, by definition, regulated by the CFTC, not the SEC as an investment vehicle. Under CFTC rules, such funds are considered commodity pools.

For example, the United States Oil Fund (USO) is an ETF designed to track the price movements of West Texas intermediate crude oil. Rather than owning thousands of barrels of oil, however, the ETF invests almost exclusively in futures contracts and is thus a registered commodity pool.

Not only commodities use this structure. The ProShares VIX (Chicago Board Options Exchange Volatility Index) Short-Term Futures Fund ETF (VIXY) and the VIX Mid-Term Futures ETF (VIXM), and other funds tracking rolled futures indexes, are also commodity pools. The VIX measures the expected volatility of the S&P 500, but there is no way to invest in it. Instead, volatility exposure is achieved through the use of VIX futures.

Commodity pools, which live solely under the umbrella of the 1933 Act, have no independent boards or similar regulatory protections that are afforded under the 1940 Act. Commodity pools are taxed as limited partnerships by the US IRS and are thus subject to unique tax treatment. We discuss the tax implications of ETFs in Chapter 5.

Exchange-Traded Notes. Finally, we use the term "ETF" to refer also to exchange-traded notes. ETNs are not truly "funds" at all; they are unsecured debt obligations of the institution that issues them. They are structured as a promise to pay a pattern of returns based on the return of the stated index minus management fees. The issuer of the note takes responsibility for setting up whatever counterbalancing hedges it believes are necessary to meet those obligations.

ETNs, like ETFs, are traded on exchanges, but they are registered under the Securities Act of 1933 because they are general obligation debt securities of a bank and are not managed by an investment firm for a fee. Holders of ETNs do not have voting rights because ETNs are debt securities.

ETNs have the largest potential counterparty risk of all exchange-traded products because they are unsecured unsubordinated debt notes. In effect, they are similar to corporate debt, except that most ETN issuers are on standby to exchange the note for intrinsic value with a notice period of a day. Theoretically, should an issuing bank declare bankruptcy, any ETNs issued by the bank would be effectively worthless. Because baskets of notes may be redeemed back to the issuer at NAV, however, typically on a daily basis (like shares of an ETF), an extremely rapid and catastrophic failure would be required to catch investors by surprise.

When Lehman Brothers defaulted in 2008, it had three ETNs on the market. Any investors still holding the ETNs when they stopped trading lost nearly all their money. Most reasonably aware investors knew Lehman was headed for difficulty, however, and had substantial time to liquidate their shares on the open market in prior weeks.

ETNs offer two distinct advantages in exchange for this counterparty risk. The first is exposure: ETNs can open up unique areas of the market or allow strategies where physically transacting in and settling the underlying securities each day would be difficult. As long as a price discovery process exists, notes can be based on an index. The issuer in launching the ETN assesses the hedging risks of making a daily market at the close based on the index level. The issuer may have an ability to manage this risk through its global trading operations, whereas investors cannot easily access the exposure directly. This ability allows complex investments or those that are difficult to manage to become investable through an ETN, often (although not always) with zero tracking error.

The second potential advantage of ETNs is taxation. Under current interpretations, the IRS considers ETNs prepaid forward contracts. So, investors do not recognize capital gains or losses until the sale or redemption of their own shares. Also, typically, ETNs do not entail dividends or interest to declare as taxable income. In certain asset classes, including commodities, ETNs can have significantly better long-term tax treatment than competing ETFs. In addition, an ETN never pays out capital gains; the pattern of returns is delivered solely through the note.

5. Evaluating ETFs: Efficiency

Perhaps the most important question an investor can ask about an ETF investment is this: Does the fund deliver on its promise?

The best ETFs closely track the indexes on which they are based and charge low and predictable investment costs. These funds provide complete, accurate information in their prospectuses and marketing materials, thus making understandable the funds' structure, composition, performance, and risks. Additionally, the best funds provide investors with the lowest possible tax exposure for the investment objective and are devoid of hidden risks.

To evaluate a fund's efficiency, each of these concepts needs to be explored.

Expense Ratio Patterns and Trends

When ETF expense ratios are compared with those of mutual funds, ETF ratios are, on average, lower. This result should be expected because ETF providers do not have to do in-house accounting or account for marketing costs, which mutual funds must do. But not all ETFs cost the same for issuers to manage; depending on their methodology, liquidity, and composition, some ETFs are more expensive than others, even if they are tracking the same index. In that case, deciding which fund to choose may come down to which one has the lowest expense ratio—because no matter what, those expenses eat into a fund's returns.

Because most ETFs are index based, expense ratios have been one of the few areas of competitive differentiation for many firms, which has led to a continuous—and investor-friendly—overall decline in fees. According to the Investment Company Institute, the average mutual fund carries an expense ratio of nearly 1.40%. **Figure 5.1** reveals a pattern in average ETF expense ratios at Q1 2014.

Because those average numbers include complex and expensive funds, however, they dramatically overstate the low cost of accessing the most typical investment strategies and indexes via ETFs. ETF investors can gain access to broad-based US equities with an expense ratio of 0.04%, to emerging market equities for 0.14%, and to US bonds for 0.05%. The pricing for accessing traditional, market-capitalization beta at the low end of the ETF cost spectrum is truly impressive.

Figure 5.1. Average Expense Ratio by Asset Class, 31 March 2014

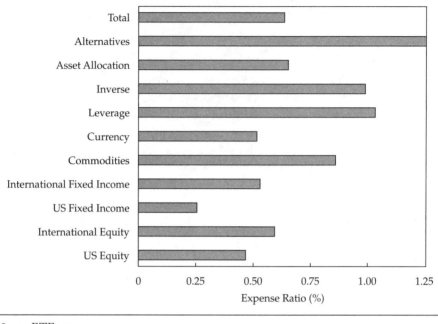

Source: ETF.com.

Tracking Error: The Rest of the Story

Looking only at stated management fees gives a false impression, however, of an ETF's true costs. What truly matters is the amount by which ETF performance lags or exceeds its benchmark index over the investor's expected (or actual) holding period. This deviation depends on a number of factors, including the fee charged by the ETF, the process and skill of the ETF's investment manager, and financial market volatility at the point of purchase and sale as it affects the bid–offer spread.

Background. Traditionally, the success of an ETF manager in achieving returns as close as possible to those of the benchmark (after subtracting fees) has been measured primarily by tracking error. Tracking error is a measurement of how closely a portfolio tracks a known pattern of returns—typically, a static index.

The most common way to assess tracking error is to examine the daily performance difference between the index and the fund tracking it. For illustration, we can look at the daily performance difference between the Vanguard FTSE Emerging Markets ETF (VWO) and its benchmark, the

FTSE Emerging Market Index, during the past three years, as shown in **Figure 5.2**.

VWO holds a cap-weighted basket of stocks designed to track the FTSE Emerging Market, which consists of the largest stocks in more than 20 emerging equity markets. The closing price of VWO is determined by the closing prices of the underlying stocks and the fact that these markets are closed when the ETF closing prices are set on US exchanges.

A reported tracking error figure is typically only the annualized standard deviation of the daily differential returns of the ETF and its benchmark. For VWO and its benchmark over the period shown, the standard deviation of daily differences is 0.18%, which annualizes to 2.81%. This annualized tracking error is high, in reflection of the complexity of the underlying asset class—equities in 20 emerging markets—as well as the time zone differences.

Unfortunately, the examination we have just done is where most published analyses stop. That 2.81% tracking error does not actually tell investors much about what kind of return they can expect, whether the fund is over- or underperforming its index, or how frequent outliers are for different holding periods. If we were the buyers on the day the fund outperformed its index by 6% and the sellers on the day it underperformed by 6%, our experience would certainly be dramatic, but most investors have much less volatile experiences. A more investor-centric way of thinking about tracking error is to look at how an average investor would experience holding the fund for a particular time

Figure 5.2. VWO Daily Tracking of FTSE Emerging Market Index, Three-Year Period Ending 31 March 2014

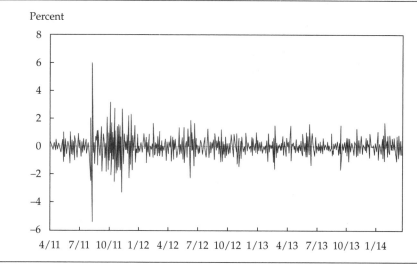

period—for instance, a year. The rolling one-year return differences between VWO and its index, as shown in **Figure 5.3**, provide a much more nuanced and informative picture than the daily return differences.

With this return difference dataset, we can get meaningful statistics, ones that most investors can understand: The mean holding period difference was –0.34%, which corresponds somewhat well to the fund's expense ratio. It would be the normal expectation for performance deviation in a year's time. In the worst 12-month holding period, however, the fund trailed its index by 3.34%; in the best, it outperformed its index by 2.60%—wild deviations that also appear on the daily differences chart. The deviations are probably driven more by overnight market moves and the delay in calculating net asset value than by any real managerial issues. The important feature is that every investor's experience for the past three years, assuming they were working with a 12-month holding period, is captured in this rolling return assessment.

Such an analysis will also lay bare any hidden costs in the portfolio— perhaps the persistent impact of portfolio rebalancing expenses or swap fees. These statistics offer a more complete picture of our investment outcome than did the expense ratio.

Figure 5.3. 12-Month Rolling Performance Difference between VWO and Its Index, March 2012–March 2014

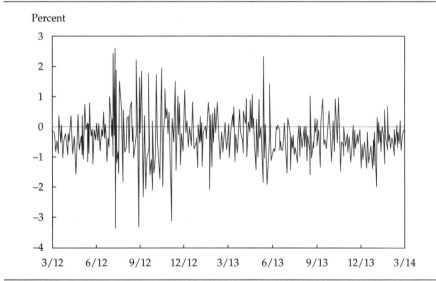

Evaluating Tracking Error. How do funds end up performing differently from their indexes, and how can investors mitigate the risk of a surprise difference in performance in their ETF investments? Beyond fees, which are known in advance, the most common source of performance differences from the fund benchmark (i.e., the tracking error) is representative sampling. The index tracked by VWO, for example, contains hundreds of securities, many of which are extremely small and illiquid, in a particular country. Actually buying all those securities would be difficult and costly. To take the theoretical index and create an actual investable product, therefore, investment managers buy only a sample of the securities in the index.

For this reason, two funds that track the exact same index may have quite different performance results. Such was the case for two popular ETFs tracking the MSCI Emerging Markets Index (EMI)—VWO and the iShares MSCI Emerging Markets ETF (EEM)—from 2010 through 2012. The MSCI is a complex, multicurrency, international index containing hundreds of illiquid securities. The performance of the two ETFs is shown in **Figure 5.4**.

In the three-year period shown in Figure 5.4, VWO—an ETF that fully replicated the target index, buying every single security in the basket—outperformed EEM, which relied heavily on representative sampling, by more

Figure 5.4. VWO vs. EEM, 31 December 2009–31 December 2012

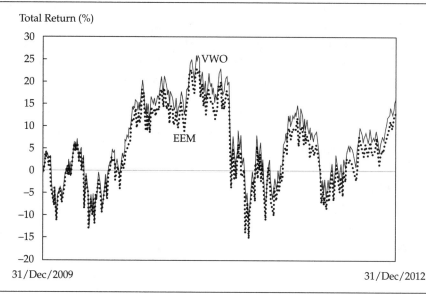

than 3.05%. Of course, representative sampling does not always work against investors. It is always, however, a source of potential tracking error.[11]

Not all tracking error is easy to predict or explain. The reality of index investing is that, no matter how sophisticated the issuer's trading desk, it will never precisely match the purely theoretical perfection of an index model, which does not have to take into account the actual messiness of buying, selling, and owning securities in a regulated market.

Additional sources of tracking error may include the following:

- *Changes to the underlying index securities.* Periodically, an index may need to be changed in some way to comply with the rules set out in its structure or because the index provider believes the index no longer represents the sector accurately. Securities may be added or deleted, or the relative weighting of a security may be increased or decreased. When such changes happen, the ETF that tracks that index may also need to make changes—especially if it follows a full replication methodology. These changes do not happen instantaneously, and the lag and costs of trading can contribute to tracking error.

- *Volatility in the ETF's asset class or specific underlying securities.* The more volatile the market, the wider the bid–offer spread and range of traded prices around NAV. Price discovery can be like trying to hit a target from a rocking boat—the bigger the waves, the more difficult to land the mark. If the stock, bond, or commodity market is experiencing high volatility with an overwhelming number of sellers (or buyers), market makers face great risks of taking the other side of these positions as they experience the high volatility in their inventory holdings. They may end up holding positions for a long time when major order imbalances occur. In extreme cases, ETFs may actually lead the underlying securities and themselves perform the price discovery process because they are easier to hedge and have more two-way order flow than the underlying securities. An increase in volatility may occur for a specific type of ETF, even though the overall market is experiencing normal volatility conditions, around earnings announcement periods in a sector, credit events in fixed income, or specific commodity market disruptions.

- *Regulatory or tax requirements.* Just as an index may need to be modified because of its underlying rules, changes in regulations may force a change

---

[11]After the period shown in Figure 5.4, Vanguard changed the index that VWO tracks to the FTSE Emerging Markets, so the two funds no longer match each other perfectly; in addition, iShares has moved to a strategy for EEM that more fully replicates its index. EEM tracking has improved significantly.

in index holdings, which may or may not affect the index being tracked. For example, for many years, Brazil imposed a tax on foreign investments coming into the country, which made perfect tracking challenging for some funds.

- *Fees and expenses incurred by the fund.* Indexes incur no fees and have no expenses. Any operating fees will put a drag on the return of a fund when compared with the performance of an index.

- *Artificial tracking error.* Investors evaluating tracking statistics must take great care because many factors can create artificial tracking error. For example, some ETFs (primarily from Vanguard and Van Eck) carry out a process called "fair valuing" their NAVs; that is, they adjust the NAV price to make a best guess on the fair value of securities trading in closed markets at the end of each day. When these fair-valued NAVs are compared with non-fair-valued indexes, the impression is that significant tracking error is going on, but the differences are simply an artifact of the fair valuation methodology.

Evaluating Tax Issues in ETFs

Two kinds of tax-based evaluations must be made for all ETFs: First, the investor must consider the likelihood of a fund distributing capital gains to existing shareholders. Second, the investor must consider what happens to shareholders when the investor sells the fund. These two actions are distinct, and the tax efficiency of a fund in terms of capital gains distributions has no link to its efficiency in terms of final sale.

Capital Gains Distributions. The issue of capital gains distributions affects all investors in taxable accounts. All mutual funds must distribute any realized capital gains that they generated during the year. They typically make these distributions at year-end, although they may make them quarterly or on another periodic schedule.

ETFs are said to be "tax efficient" and "tax fair" because they have certain advantages over traditional mutual funds when it comes to capital gains distributions. On average, they distribute far less in capital gains than competing mutual funds do for three primary reasons.

First, most ETFs are index funds, and index funds generate less in capital gains than actively managed products. The reason is simple: On average, index funds have significantly lower turnover than active strategies, which translates into lower gains. This advantage is being blurred by the growth of quasi-active index strategies in the ETF space, but it nonetheless exists.

Second, with ETFs, the selling activities of individual investors do not force the fund itself to trade out of positions. In a traditional mutual fund, when an investor sells, the fund must (with a few exceptions) go out into the market and sell underlying securities to raise cash to pay that investor. This process can increase turnover in the fund, which, in turn, can lead to larger gains distributions. In other words, in a traditional mutual fund, shareholders who stay in the fund may have to pay tax bills triggered by other shareholders redeeming out of the fund—and such taxation can be substantial.

In contrast, an investor in an ETF simply sells his or her ETF shares to another investor. The fund firm typically does not even know that the sale is occurring and certainly does not need to alter its portfolio to accommodate this transaction. This aspect is why ETFs are considered tax fair: The actions of investors selling shares of the fund do not influence the tax bills of shareholders who stay in the fund.

The third and most important reason arises from the way the creation/redemption mechanism works. When an authorized participant submits shares of an ETF for redemption, the ETF manager can choose which share lots it delivers to the AP in the redemption basket. Smart managers choose shares with the largest embedded capital gains. ETFs with in-kind redemption processes, by virtue of this feature, are constantly cleansing themselves of potential capital gains.

Nevertheless, capital gains are possible. For instance, if an index is tracking the S&P 500 and one of the companies is replaced, that outgoing company's stock has to be sold and the new stock purchased. If the sale price is higher than the original purchase price of the outgoing company's stock, a taxable gain occurs. Alternatively, many indexes have rebalancing periods—often quarterly but, in some cases, as often as daily—and funds tracking that index will have to mimic those changes. Each time rebalancing occurs, the chance for taxable capital gains arises.

Other triggers include mergers and acquisitions and the graduation of stocks or bonds out of a particular band. For instance, if a security moves out of the S&P Midcap 400 Index into the S&P 500, it may have to be sold in the S&P 400 ETFs.

Nonetheless, on balance, ETFs have historically been much less likely than competing mutual funds to distribute capital gains. Recall that in 2012, iShares announced it would make capital gains distributions in only 2 of its 233 ETFs.

Tax upon Sale. The second facet of tax efficiency stems from what happens when an ETF is sold. (The information in the following subsections relates to tax rates effective 1 January 2013.)

Exchange-traded products are primarily taxed according to their underlying regulatory structures. Each ETF falls into one of five regulatory structures: open-end fund, unit investment trust, grantor trust, limited partnership (LP), or exchange-traded note. A fund can also be taxed disparately according to its holdings: equities, fixed income, commodities, currencies, or alternatives.

The interplay between the regulatory structure and the asset class determines how the IRS taxes a specific ETF. In the tables in the following subsections, the tax rates given for each asset class and applicable structure are the *maximums*. The rates listed *do not* include the new Medicare surcharge tax of 3.8% applicable to certain investors. Long-term capital gains apply to positions held for longer than one year; short-term capital gains apply to positions held for one year or less.

Equity and Fixed-Income Funds. Table 5.1 displays the long-term and short-term capital gains tax rates for equity and fixed-income ETFs. Equity and fixed-income funds are treated the same with regard to taxation. The structures of equity exchange-traded products in these asset classes are open-end funds, UITs, and ETNs. (Prior to their closure in December 2011, HOLDRS funds were grantor trusts in the equity asset class.)

All three applicable structures in this asset class receive the same tax treatment. If the shares are held for less than one year, they are considered short-term investments and any gains are taxed as ordinary income, with a maximum tax rate of 39.60%. Shares held longer than a year qualify as long-term investments, and any capital gains are taxed at the long-term capital gains rate of 20%.

Table 5.1. Maximum Capital Gains Tax Rate: Equity and Fixed-Income ETFs

Structure	Long-Term Capital Gains	Short-Term Capital Gains
Open end (1940 Act)	20%	39.60%
UIT (1940 Act)	22	39.60
ETN (1933 Act)	20	39.60

Commodity Funds. Commodity funds fall into one of three structures—grantor trust, LP, or ETN—depending on the type of commodity held. Understanding the structure of the fund is critical because the tax implications vary. **Table 5.2** shows the maximum capital gains tax rates currently in effect for commodity ETFs.

Table 5.2. Maximum Capital Gains Tax Rate: Commodity ETFs

Structure	Long-Term Capital Gains	Short-Term Capital Gains
Grantor trust (1933 Act)	28.00%	39.60%
LP (1933 Act)[a]	27.84[b]	27.84[b]
ETN (1933 Act)	20.00	39.60

[a]Distributes K-1 partnership income form.
[b]Maximum rate of blended 60% long term/40% short term.

■ *Commodity grantor trusts.* A commodity fund that physically holds the commodity in question is set up as a grantor trust. The most familiar of these is the SPDR Gold Shares GLD), an ETF that physically holds gold bullion. The iShares Silver Trust (SLV) fund is another example of a commodity grantor trust; SLV holds physical silver.

Investments in these funds are treated the same as if the investor personally bought and sold the underlying physical metal. The IRS, treating all precious metal investments as collectibles, assesses a maximum rate of 28% for long-term investments and ordinary income rates (to a maximum of 39.60%) for short-term investments.

■ *Commodity LPs.* The IRS treats ETFs that hold commodity futures contracts as limited partnerships. These funds have unique tax implications, with 60% of any gains taxed at the long-term capital gains rate of 20% and the remaining 40% taxed at ordinary income tax rates (to a maximum of 39.60%). The result is a blended maximum capital gains rate of 27.84%.

Additionally, LPs receive very different tax treatment from the treatment of registered investment companies. All securities in a commodity LP are marked to market at the end of the year, and any gains based on that marking are passed on to investors to be immediately taxed. With this end-of-year cost basis adjustment, investors may owe taxes on gains even if they never sold the shares and still hold the ETF in their portfolio. These gains are reported to investors through K-1 partnership income forms, which investors may be unfamiliar with.

■ *Commodity ETNs.* Commodity ETNs do not physically hold commodities or commodity futures. They hold unsubordinated, unsecured debt notes issued by providers with a promise to provide the return of a specific index or commodity.

In contrast to the odd treatment of commodity pools, the IRS currently taxes commodity ETNs like equity and fixed-income funds. Long-term gains are taxed at 20.00%, and short-term gains are taxed as ordinary income (to a maximum of 39.60%). Furthermore, commodity ETNs avoid the mark-to-market issues associated with LP-based ETFs.

Currency Funds. Currency funds can be open-end funds, grantor trusts, LPs, or ETNs. As with commodity funds, knowing the type will help an investor understand the tax implications. In **Table 5.3**, we show the maximum capital gains rates that apply to currency holdings.

Table 5.3. Maximum Capital Gains Tax Rate: Currency ETFs

Structure	Long-Term Capital Gains	Short-Term Capital Gains
Open end (1940 Act)	20.00%	39.60%
Grantor trust (1933 Act)	40.00	39.60
LP (1933 Act)[a]	27.84[b]	27.84[b]
ETN (1933 Act)	40.00	39.60

[a]Distributes K-1 partnership income form.
[b]Maximum rate of blended 60% long term/40% short term.

■ *Currency open-end funds.* Open-end currency funds are taxed similarly to equity funds, with long-term capital gains taxed at 20.00% and short-term capital gains taxed as ordinary income (to a maximum of 39.60%).

■ *Currency grantor trusts.* A currency grantor trust holds foreign currency in foreign bank accounts to give investors exposure to spot exchange rates of the underlying currency. The deposit earns a local interest rate that accrues daily and is paid monthly as ordinary dividend income. Examples of currency grantor trusts are Rydex's CurrencyShares ETFs.

Tax rates on gains from the sale of shares in these trusts are simply treated as ordinary income (to a maximum of 39.60%), regardless of how long they were held.

■ *Currency LPs.* ETFs that hold currency futures are considered limited partnerships for tax purposes. These funds are taxed in the same way as commodity LPs, with 60% of any gains taxed at the long-term capital gains rate and the remaining 40% taxed at ordinary income tax rates. The result is a blended maximum capital gains rate of 27.84%. They are also marked to market at the end of the year and generate K-1 forms, just as their commodity brethren do.

■ *Currency ETNs.* Currency ETNs are a rare exception: The tax treatment for a currency ETN is absolutely clear. Since late 2007 when IRS Ruling 2008-1 went into effect, currency ETNs have been taxed as ordinary income, regardless of holding period. According to the prospectuses of some currency ETNs, however, investors might have an option to classify gains as long-term capital gains if a valid election under Section 988 is made before the end of the day that the ETN was purchased.

Most ETNs do not pay out any distributions to shareholders, but investors in currency ETNs are responsible for any *embedded* gains at ordinary income tax rates (to a maximum of 39.60%). This aspect gives currency ETNs one of the worst tax treatments of any investment product. Investors pay their maximum tax rate on undistributed, notional gains. This tax treatment has made it difficult for currency ETNs to find favor with investors and gain significant assets.

Alternatives. Alternative funds can be open-end funds, LPs, or ETNs. These funds attempt to provide diversification within a fund by combining asset classes or investing in nontraditional assets. **Table 5.4** provides the maximum capital gains tax rates applicable to alternatives ETFs.

Some examples of alternatives ETFs are ProShares VIX Short-Term Futures Fund (VIXY) and PowerShares S&P 500 BuyWrite (PBP). PBP is taxed like an equity fund, with long-term gains taxed at 20% and short-term gains taxed at the ordinary income rate to a maximum of 39.60%. VIXY is

Table 5.4. Maximum Capital Gains Tax Rate: Alternative Asset ETFs

Structure	Long-Term Capital Gains	Short-Term Capital Gains
Open end (1940 Act)	20.00%	39.60%
LP (1933 Act)[a]	27.84[b]	27.84[b]
ETN (1933 Act)[c]	20.00	39.60

[a]Distributes K-1 partnership income form.
[b]Maximum rate of blended 60% long term/40% short term.
[c]Exception is ticker ICI; see explanation in text.

structured as an LP, and all gains are taxed at the blended 60/40 rate, with a maximum blended rate of 27.84%. This treatment is independent of how long the fund has been held.

Alternatives that are structured as ETNs are treated the same as equity ETNs, with one exception (so far)—the iPath Optimized Currency Carry ETN (ICI) is treated as a currency ETN. Its gains are generally taxed as ordinary income, independent of how long the note has been held.

Distributions. So far, we have discussed only capital gains, but other events can trigger tax obligations, one of which is distributions. Distributions may be monthly, quarterly, semiannually, or annually and come from dividends from underlying stock holdings or interest from fixed income or other holdings.

A third form of distributions is from return of capital (ROC). ROC distributions are funds paid out in excess of an ETF's earnings and profits and serve to reduce an investor's cost basis by the amount of the distribution. These distributions are generally not taxable. These types of distributions are typically only seen in real estate investment trust ETFs and master limited partnership ETFs, although theoretically any fund can make ROC distributions.

■ *Qualified dividends vs. nonqualified dividends.* Aside from the rare ROC distribution or capital gains distribution, dividend distributions are the most common kind of distribution ETF investors will experience. The key question for dividends is whether they are qualified or nonqualified.

Qualified dividends come from a US company whose shares have been held by the ETF for more than 60 days during the 121-day period that begins 60 days before the ex-dividend date. Nonqualified dividends are payments that fail this test. Qualified dividends are taxed at a maximum rate of 20%, whereas nonqualified dividends are taxed as ordinary income.

Bond ETFs often call their monthly distributions of interest payments "dividends," but these payouts are not considered qualified dividends and are taxed as ordinary income. Other interest-yielding funds, such as certain currency funds, also have their distributions taxed as ordinary income. Similarly, revenue from such activities as security lending is always treated as ordinary income.

No matter in what way the distributions are treated, they should be broken down in the 1099-DIV at year-end as follows:

- "Total Ordinary Dividends" includes both qualified and nonqualified dividends plus short-term capital gains.

- "Qualified Dividends" covers any dividends that qualify for the 20% tax rate.

- "Total Capital Gains Distributions" contains any long-term capital gains that qualify for the 20% tax rate.

- "Non-Dividend Distributions" should contain any ROC distributions.

Most ETFs are good at managing the dividend stream to ensure that payments are predominantly qualified, but certain ETFs—particularly fast-growing or new funds—can run into problems.

■ *New Medicare surcharge tax.* Effective 1 January 2013 with passage of the Patient Protection and Affordable Care Act, single individuals with an adjusted gross income (AGI) more than $200,000 and married taxpayers filing jointly with an AGI more than $250,000 are now subject to an additional 3.8% Medicare surcharge tax on investment income, which includes all capital gains, interest, and dividends.

This new tax is levied on the lesser of (1) net investment income or (2) modified AGI in excess of $200,000 single/$250,000 joint. Therefore, for investors in the highest tax brackets, their "true" tax rates on long-term capital gains and qualified dividends can reach 23.8% (20% capital gains plus 3.8% Medicare tax).

Understanding ETF Risks

Any investment has market risk, but ETFs can introduce several unique sources of risk that may be unfamiliar to a traditional stock-and-bond investor as to both the instruments' structure and holding type.

Expectation-Related Risk. Perhaps the greatest strength of ETFs is that they provide to a broad range of investors, large and small, access to asset classes and investment strategies that had previously been limited to the large institutional investors or investors that were familiar with derivative products. Some of these asset classes and strategies are sophisticated, however, and many investors are not familiar with them. Proper use of these unfamiliar ETFs in a portfolio requires education of investors if they are to fully understand the return and risk features. Therefore, the biggest risk of investing in ETFs may simply be one of misunderstanding what the ETF is, how it works, and how it will perform.

Leveraged and inverse funds are the clearest case in point. Most funds offering levered, inverse, or levered-and-inverse exposure to a given index have a daily objective that is a multiple of index returns. That is, they reset their exposure daily to be in line with that day's target multiple of returns. Thus, a fund offering 200% exposure to the S&P 500 delivers that doubled exposure for one day and then resets its basis to "200% invested" for the following day. If you hold the fund for longer than that period, the math of compounding is such that you will not see a straight 200% return over the full term. In volatile markets with low returns in the full period, the holding period returns can be below the multiplier times the benchmark because of the way the portfolio rebalances daily. In other circumstances, this rebalancing to meet the daily multiplier objective can augment the return to a level higher than the multiple times the benchmark.

Figure 5.5 shows how leveraged and inverse funds can vary from their daily objective multiplier over long holding periods. The two ETFs are the Direxion Daily Financial Bull 3X Shares (FAS) and Direxion Daily Financial Bear 3X Shares (FAZ), which follow the Russell 1000 Financials Index. During the course of 2010—a volatile year for the financial markets—the Russell 1000 Financials ended the year up slightly under 12%. The bull-market FAS tracking this index ended up 13% on the year. However, if the investor did not understand the daily objective feature, a 3X FAS investor

Figure 5.5. Compounding Impact on Daily Objective Multiplier ETF Returns: FAS and FAZ, 31 December 2009–31 December 2010

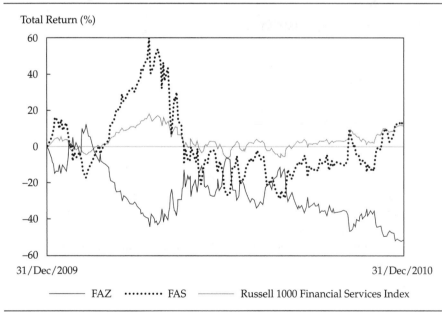

might have expected a 35% return rather than 12% that the ETF provided to a buy-and-hold investor who did not rebalance.

Trending markets have less of a compounding effect than volatile markets. Around midyear 2010 when the Russell 1000 Financials was up slightly under 20%, the bull-market 3X ETF FAS was up close to 3 times, or 60%, because the market was in a trending pattern.

As a result of these compounding effects in leveraged (geared) ETFs, the funds are generally not intended to be buy-and-hold products for more than a one-month horizon. If investors are going to hold them long term, they must rebalance the funds periodically to maintain the desired net exposure.

Fund fact sheets and prospectuses clearly state the risks, and other resources, such as Direxion.com and ProShares.com, have documentation and tools to explain the ins and outs of these funds and how they behave in various scenarios.

Similarly, investors in commodity ETFs may not be familiar with the striking impact that contango and backwardation, the patterns in prices of futures expiring at different dates, can have on their portfolios. Some people may buy a crude oil ETF expecting to earn the return of spot crude oil prices, but the funds are actually benchmarked to rolled positions in crude oil futures. The returns are, therefore, based on expected crude oil spot prices on a futures expiration date and also reflect the cost or benefit of rolling out of an expiring futures contract and into the next month's future. For example, in the 12-month period ending 30 September 2013, the most popular crude oil ETF—the United States Oil Fund, LP (USO)—returned 8%, whereas spot crude was up 11%. Again, the associated risks were clearly detailed in the prospectus, but some investors may have been caught unaware.

Ultimately, these risks are all variants of basis risk and are inherent aspects of investing in a particular asset class or strategy. We explore some of the asset class–specific issues in Part II, starting with Chapter 8, of this book.

Structural Risk. Only one ETF structure, the ETN, carries with it a different level of structural risk than other common investment products. The unique structure of ETNs as unsubordinated, unsecured debt opens them up to the risk of credit default by the note holder (issuer). Theoretically, the counterparty risk is 100%. An informed investor should have time to sell out of an ETN investment before the underwriting bank defaults, but anything less than close monitoring introduces significant risk.

Evaluating this counterparty risk can be difficult, and various measures are used. One of the simplest means of staying apprised of this risk is to monitor the market's own proxy for the banks' default risks—credit default swaps (CDS). As of the end of Q1 2014, all ETN counterparties had active CDS contracts. The credit spreads for one-year CDS by issuer as of the end of March 2013 are shown in **Figure 5.6**.

The quoted CDS rates are the cost to insure debt, in basis points per year; so, for example, investors could "insure" $1 million in Goldman Sachs bonds for a little under $40,000 per year. Although the insurance rate should never be considered an estimate of actual default risk for a 12-month period, it does provide a good gauge of the relative risk of the various issuers. In general, a one-year CDS rate above 5% should raise significant concerns among investors because it foretells a significant default risk in the year to come.

Another risk of ETNs is the risk that the issuer of the note may halt creations and redemptions when the issuer decides it does not wish to add to the debt on its balance sheet related to the index on which the ETN is based. This risk is a business risk of the ETN issuer and may be driven by concerns about the ease or cost of hedging the exposure or simply the size of the issue related to the amount of other debt outstanding. A recent example of an ETN issuer halting creations was the case of the VelocityShares 2X VIX Short-Term ETN (TVIX); it was halted for several weeks in early 2012. The ETN traded at a large premium to the underlying VIX futures and to other similar ETFs during this time.

Figure 5.6. One-Year CDS Spreads for ETN Issuers, 31 March 2014

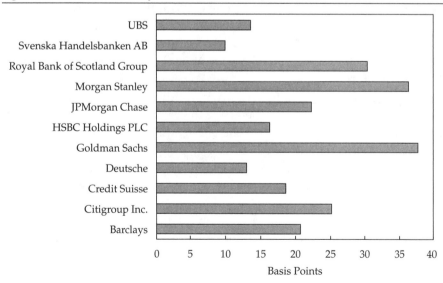

Holdings-Based Risk. ETNs are not the only products that take on counterparty risk. The type of holdings a fund has can open it up to some risk as well. A fund that uses derivatives, such as swaps, to gain exposure to a market has some level of counterparty risk. For example, the Market Vectors China A Shares ETF (PEK) uses swaps to gain exposure to the Chinese market. Swaps are not as risky as an ETN, but investors still need to understand what is going on in such an ETF.

In a swap agreement, two parties agree to exchange a pattern of returns for a fee. For example, a major bank might agree to provide Van Eck with exposure to Chinese A-shares for a fee. In the beginning, no money changes hands. Instead, an account is created that must be balanced on the basis of movements in the referenced index. If the Chinese market goes up, the swap counterparty will have to put in cash to reflect that movement in value. If the market goes down, Van Eck will put money in. Accounts are typically settled frequently—usually on a daily or weekly basis. This frequent settlement reduces the damage the swap partners face if a company goes bankrupt.

The ETF holder is exposed to the credit risk of the issuer of the swap only on the return of the index since the last time the swap reset or exchanged cash with the swap counterparty. Most swaps in ETFs reset daily, so this credit risk is only intraday. Also, the bulk of the funds invested in an ETF are held in cash equivalents, such as US T-bills at a custodian bank. Only the daily returns (or returns between reset dates) on the swap are exposed to the counterparty risk.

Although understanding the risks associated with swaps is important, swap exposures are not unique to ETFs. Many mutual funds also use swaps and other derivatives to gain exposures. With ETFs, at least that exposure is transparent.

Similarly, ETF issuers (together with traditional mutual fund managers and institutions) commonly lend out their underlying securities to short sellers as a way of earning extra income for investors. Securities lent out are generally overcollateralized, to 102%, and the risk from counterparty default is too small to be of concern. When funds have lost money in securities lending arrangements, the loss has come from the way a fund reinvested that collateral.

A well-run securities lending program can bring in money and offset the expenses of running the fund. Information about these lending programs tends to be scanty, however, and poorly disclosed. Investors should, at a minimum, be aware of how their funds are using their money.

Fund-Closure Risk. As with a mutual fund, issuers can decide that an ETF no longer makes sense and shut it down. Such a fund closing does not result in an outright loss for investors; funds simply sell off positions and return cash to investors. But the resulting activity can affect investors negatively through capital gains distributions (forced realized gains because the closure of the fund creates a tax event for the shareholder) and the hassle of finding a new investment vehicle. In a few cases, investors have been stuck with the fees and costs associated with a fund's closure.

The primary reasons a fund closes have to do with regulation, competition, and corporate activity.

■ *Regulations.* As the ETF environment changes, regulatory bodies change with it. Securities regulators can decide to change the regulations governing certain types of funds, resulting in forced closure of those funds. Commodity futures are under constant scrutiny by regulators, for instance, and position limits can make it impossible for some funds to function.

These regulatory issues are generally well documented on websites and in newsletters tracking the ETF industry, and most providers believe they will be able to continue operating under the current proposals being discussed. The situation is fluid, however, and could change at any time.

■ *Competition.* The growing number of ETFs means increased competition. In addition, the bigger the field, the more likely that some funds will fail to attract investor assets and will shut down. Investors should look at the assets under management of the fund they are interested in and the AUM of its competitors to see how robust the fund is. Another measurement of the health of a fund is how interested the rest of the market is in it. If the average daily dollar volume is high, the market is interested. A dearth of both AUM and volume for a significant period should be a red flag that a fund could be facing elimination.

■ *Corporate actions.* As a young and fast-growing industry, the ETF space commonly experiences mergers and acquisitions. When fund families change hands, the implications are not always obvious. Generally, new owners will prune underperforming ETFs (from an asset-gathering perspective) and invest in new, higher-growth opportunities.

6. Evaluating ETFs: Trading

ETFs, like stocks, are accessed on exchanges, through a brokerage account—that is, via financial advisers or institutional sales teams of registered broker/dealers or through on-line transaction services. Trading is one of the largest differences between ETFs and open-end mutual funds, which are purchased and sold once a day at the closing net asset value of the fund holdings. Mutual fund transactions are done through phone or internet communication directly with the mutual fund management firm by either the investor or his or her financial adviser or discount broker.

An ETF has the advantage that it can be purchased whenever exchanges are open—as well as at closing NAV when a transaction is large enough to qualify for a creation or redemption. As with all exchange-traded products, ETF investors usually need to pay a commission, however, and incur a trading cost related to the liquidity factors associated with the ETF. The trading costs include the bid–ask spread, the size of the trade relative to the normal trading activity of the ETF, and the ease of hedging the ETF by the market-making community. In this chapter, we discuss the factors that relate to the trading features of ETFs, how to compare ETFs that differ in liquidity, and the importance in trading costs of the liquidity of the underlying index holdings of an ETF.

Trading Costs: Part of the Overall Expense of Investing in ETFs

Much focus has been on the rapid growth of ETFs in terms of assets, especially in contrast to mutual funds, but ETFs have also grown to become a significant component of exchange trading activity. Since 2007 in the United States, ETFs have consistently represented between 15% and 25% of the total dollar value traded when aggregated with equity trading activity. **Figure 6.1** charts ETF trading activity in shares as a percentage of consolidated tape volume and as a percentage of the dollar value traded over the 12-month period from April 2013 to March 2014.

Note that ETF trading is dominated by the largest ETFs in terms of assets. **Table 6.1** shows the largest 15 ETFs as of 31 March 2014 together with their asset size, average dollar volume over the prior 60 days, and median daily volume as a percentage of assets.

The percentage of assets that trade on a typical trading day, as shown in Table 6.1 for the largest US-traded ETFs, provides an indication of liquidity relative to the size of the fund. A high percentage typically means that the

©2015 The CFA Institute Research Foundation

Figure 6.1. ETF Trading Activity as a Percentage of US Equity Trading, 1 April 2013–27 March 2014

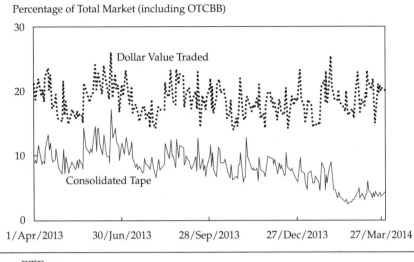

Percentage of Total Market (including OTCBB)

Source: ETF.com.

Table 6.1. Assets, Volume, and Daily Turnover of the Largest ETFs, Q1 2014

Ticker	Name	Issuer	AUM ($ millions)	Median Daily Volume ($ millions)	Percent of AUM
SPY	SPDR S&P 500	SSgA	157,180	23,137	14.72
IVV	iShares Core S&P 500	BlackRock	54,367	1,023	1.88
EFA	iShares MSCI EAFE	BlackRock	53,956	1,358	2.52
QQQ	PowerShares QQQ	Invesco PowerShares	43,937	3,486	7.93
VWO	Vanguard FTSE Emerging Markets	Vanguard	42,393	760	1.79
VTI	Vanguard Total Stock Market	Vanguard	41,449	296	0.71
GLD	SPDR Gold	SSgA	33,753	1,068	3.16
EEM	iShares MSCI Emerging Markets	BlackRock	31,884	3,065	9.61
IWM	iShares Russell 2000	BlackRock	28,814	5,496	19.07
IWF	iShares Russell 1000 Growth	BlackRock	22,993	188	0.82

(continued)

Table 6.1.   Assets, Volume, and Daily Turnover of the Largest ETFs, Q1 2014
(continued)

Ticker	Name	Issuer	AUM ($ millions)	Median Daily Volume ($ millions)	Percent of AUM
IWD	iShares Russell 1000 Value	BlackRock	21,287	165	0.77
VNQ	Vanguard REIT	Vanguard	21,005	283	1.35
VEA	Vanguard FTSE Developed Markets	Vanguard	20,802	147	0.71
IJH	iShares Core S&P Mid-Cap	BlackRock	20,641	205	1.00
BND	Vanguard Total Bond Market	Vanguard	19,381	185	0.95
VIG	Vanguard Dividend Appreciation	Vanguard	18,919	83	0.44
XLF	Financial Select SPDR	SSgA	18,693	1,028	5.50
VOO	Vanguard S&P 500	Vanguard	16,703	209	1.25
LQD	iShares iBoxx $ Investment Grade Corporate Bond	BlackRock	16,625	174	1.04
AGG	iShares Core U.S. Aggregate Bond	BlackRock	16,181	124	0.77

Source: ETF.com (as of 31 March 2014).

ETF is used extensively for tactical trading, even though some of the investors hold for longer horizons.[12] Among the largest ETFs, by far the most liquid relative to their assets are SPY and IWM on, respectively, the S&P 500 and Russell 2000 Indexes, where daily turnover can be 15%–20% of their asset values. IVV is the second-largest ETF in assets but trades only about 2% of its assets daily, so it is used more by long-horizon investors. SPY and IVV have the same underlying index—the S&P 500—but SPY is structured as a unit investment trust and thus does not reinvest dividends between ex-dividend dates, whereas IVV, as a registered investment company, does

---

[12]Liquidity for an ETF with a lower percentage of assets trading daily can still be good if the underlying securities are liquid or if the ETF is similar to a very active ETF that can be used for hedging by market makers.

reinvest between the dates. Both are liquid, with tight bid–offer spreads, but investors with different trading styles and horizons prefer different funds, as indicated by the ratio.

Another example is EEM compared with VWO. Both funds are large and liquid, but EEM tends to have a tighter bid–ask spread and has holdings that are more liquid than VWO. EEM had a median daily volume of about 10% of its assets, whereas VWO typically trades only 2% of its assets. So, EEM has a greater portion of its assets and trading activity coming from short-horizon investors. The liquidity is one factor that would be considered by investors choosing between the two ETFs; other factors would be the fit of the index to the investment objective, the fees, the dividend income, and structural differences (none in this case because they are both 1940 Act funds).

Note that the largest fixed-income ETFs, such as BND, LQD, and AGG, trade only a small percentage of their assets daily, typically 1% or less. This percentage indicates that most fixed-income ETF investors are using them less for tactical trading purposes than as a low-cost, efficient means of investing in a broadly diversified portfolio of fixed-income securities.

Keep in mind when evaluating the costs of ETFs that expected trading costs and management fees paid to the fund sponsor should be considered. Both of these cost components depend on the expected holding period. The longer a position is held, the more management fees matter because the investor pays them year after year. Trading costs are incurred only at the purchase and sale. Trading costs are not as critical for ETF investors with long time horizons as for active short-term investors. For those short-term investors however, management fees may be less relevant in light of the cost of entering and exiting the position.

Note that mutual funds pay transaction costs also, but they pay them inside the body of the fund itself as the manager buys and sells securities to deal with investor cash flows. With mutual funds, trades associated with net inflows and outflows are executed by the fund portfolio manager and the costs are aggregated across all flows of the mutual fund on the day the inflow or outflow occurs. The trading costs of net inflows and outflows represent a reduction in the returns of the mutual fund and affect the performance of all investors in the fund. These costs are not visible to the mutual fund investors. With ETFs, the trading costs incurred are explicit and paid by the investor when accessing the ETF transaction on an exchange.

Trading Costs vs. Management Fees by Holding Period

To illustrate the relative size of management fees versus trading costs in ETF investing, imagine we pay a commission of $100 on a $40,000 trade (0.25% each way, or 0.50% total) combined with a 0.10% bid–offer spread on purchase and sale. The total is a roundtrip trading cost of 0.60%. Even if our round trip happens in a year, this 0.60% can be much larger than the annual expenses of many ETFs. If held for less than a year, these costs will likely overwhelm the expense ratio of the ETF.

Consider 3-month versus 12-month or three-year holding period costs on an ETF with a 0.24% annual fee, commissions of 0.50%, and a bid–ask spread of 0.10%. As illustrated in **Figure 6.2**, total expenses would be 0.66% for a 3-month position and 0.84% for a 12-month position. Excluding the compounding effect, they could be as high as 1.32% [0.60% + (3 × 0.24%)] for a three-year holding period. Commissions can represent a big part of the ETF cost on a low-fee ETF, but the longer the ETF is held, the greater the proportion of total costs that accrue to the management fee component.

ETF sponsors that also have brokerage arms have begun competing aggressively for investor flows. Some are offering trading with no commissions to attract investor funds into their complexes and earn management fees. The brokerage arms of Vanguard and Schwab, for example, charge no commissions on ETFs they manage. Schwab, Fidelity, and TD Ameritrade have also negotiated arrangements with a group of ETF managers to offer commission-free trading through their brokerage platforms.

Figure 6.2. Example of ETF Management Fee and Trading Costs for Various Holding Periods

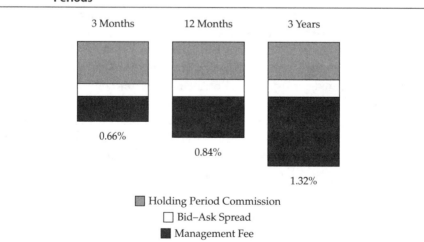

Comparing the overall impact of trading costs on ETF returns with the impact on mutual fund returns is difficult. With ETFs, entry and exit incurs a commission and one leg of the trading spread, but the strategies themselves, being largely index based, tend to have lower turnover than many mutual funds, which are typically actively managed. With mutual funds, the fund manager will invest new inflows that come in at the NAV, but the trading costs of investing these funds will simply be a reduction in total fund returns, like any other cost the fund might incur from trading. Mutual funds typically pay institutional commission rates because of their size; depending on the brokerage relationship, a retail investor may find ETF commissions higher for small transactions.[13] From the end investor's perspective, however, the issue of cost in ETF investing is simple: The cost of buying and selling falls to the investor, not the investment manager. Whether the investor considers that deal fair requires a thoughtful analysis of the total cost of ownership—and smart trading.

And what is smart trading in ETFs? As a rule, ETFs that trade actively and have narrow bid–ask spreads (0.05% or less) can be easily executed electronically for orders of under 10,000 shares. Because prices can move quickly, however, limit orders should always be used in ETF trading. Recently executed trades and advertised bid–ask spread quotes should be used as a guide for choosing the limit price.[14] For large orders or for ETFs for which trading is less active, financial advisers and institutional investors can get advice and assistance on trading strategies from their brokerage firms' ETF desks or from the capital market specialist teams at the ETF sponsors. Low ETF average or median volume should not discourage investors from considering an ETF. As long as the liquidity of the securities or derivatives in the underlying index is adequate, the ETF can usually be executed in a cost-effective way. The capital market specialists at ETF managers and broker/dealer ETF desks offer assistance to investors to help them understand the various execution options and potential trading costs of buying or selling an ETF with the assistance of a liquidity provider. For small, retail investors, however, ETFs should be viewed through the lens of onscreen liquidity, and illiquid ETFs should be traded with the same caution afforded a microcap stock.

---

[13]Moreover, keep in mind that ETFs involve two sets of commissions and spreads: one internal to the fund's operations, the second resulting from the end investor's need to buy and sell the ETF shares in the open market. "No-load" mutual funds involve only one set of commissions and spreads—those arising from the fund's internal operations.

[14]Because of the "Flash Crash" of 2010 and other factors, some experts advise retail investors to use limit orders for all stock as well as ETF trades.

The Primary Market for ETFs: Creation, Redemption, and the Authorized Participant

The previous sections dealt with how end investors purchase and sell shares of ETFs on the open market. None of that activity, however, actually puts money into the hands of the investment managers of the ETFs themselves. As discussed in Chapter 3, every ETF has authorized participants, which are US-registered self-clearing brokerage firms that have agreements with the ETF manager or distributor to create and redeem ETF shares at the NAV price at the end of each day.

If the market price of the ETF departs from the NAV to a greater extent than the cost of buying or selling the underlying ETF holdings, the AP can buy (sell) the "mispriced" ETF in the open market and redeem (create) it at NAV with the issuer. Creations and redemptions can be done for cash but are more commonly done "in-kind," meaning an AP who creates or redeems ETF shares with the issuer will receive the underlying securities of the ETF on redemption or will need to provide new underlying securities in a creation. This creation/redemption window at the end of each trading session is the mechanism by which funds flow to and from the fund manager. With creation and redemption, ETFs function similarly to mutual funds; the difference is that only APs can create and redeem shares at NAV, and there is a minimum number of shares per creation or redemption.

The monitoring of whether the secondary market price of the ETF is "fair," and of the opportunity to earn an arbitrage profit, is the key to keeping ETFs trading close to fair value (a topic covered in more depth later in the discussion of premiums and discounts). But the extent to which ETFs trade close to fair value is limited by the liquidity and trading costs of the underlying securities. If the creation basket for a fund contains securities that are extremely hard to acquire, the AP will allow the price to drift substantially from NAV before acting to book the arbitrage. That action will show up in the form of wider quote spreads, which adds to the investor's total cost.

To combat this, some issuers resort to cash creations and redemptions, effectively internalizing the costs of acquiring new securities (as in a traditional mutual fund). This practice is particularly common in fixed-income ETFs, where substantial expertise is often required to execute trades efficiently. Other issuers will pursue a hybrid approach, either using a mixture of easy-to-trade securities and cash or using cash creations but in-kind redemptions.

The Secondary Market for ETFs: The Bid–Ask Spread

Because the average investor cannot interact directly with the issuer, the primary market, he or she buys and sells ETFs in the secondary markets—that is, the stock market. Like stocks, ETF shares are quoted at an "ask" or "offer" price for those who are buying and at a lower "bid" price for investors interested in selling. The bid–ask spread is the gap between those prices. For the most liquid ETFs, spreads are usually narrow—often only a few cents—but small, less active ETFs can have much larger bid–ask spreads. The tighter the spread, the lower the cost to trade the shares because the difference the market maker is charging between the buying and selling price is less.

The bid–ask spread, like the commission level, is of more concern to frequent traders than to investors with a long-term investment strategy. Nevertheless, a wide bid–ask spread can eat into overall returns. A bid–ask spread is always expressed with an amount to trade at the indicative bid and offer. Typically, when an investor gets an electronic quote from a broker, the investor sees the bid and offer for a small order size—usually 100 shares. By going to a market maker or ETF desk, the investor can get a bid–ask quote for any order size. Larger trades relative to the volume of the ETF and underlying securities have wide bid–ask spreads. From time to time, imbalances occur in the amount supplied and demanded so the spread can be tilted to favor buyers or sellers. For example, in a rapidly declining equity market, where sellers are dominating the order flow, a request for a large quote might yield an ask price closer to the fair value and a bid price further away from fair value.

The primary factors that determine the width of a bid–ask spread are the amount of ongoing order flow (more flow means lower spreads), the amount of competition among market makers for that ETF (more competition means lower spreads), and the actual costs and risks associated with an AP doing the creation/redemption process. These costs and risks include creation/redemption fees, the bid–ask spread of the underlying securities in the ETF basket, brokerage fees, currency-hedging costs, and the risk of hedging exposures until the AP can actually do the creation or redemption. Beyond these costs, market makers and APs will have some level of profit margin they expect to achieve from being in the market in the first place.

Put another way, ETF bid–ask spreads are generally less than or equal to the combination of the following:

±   Creation/redemption and other direct costs

+   Bid–ask spread of underlying securities

+   Risk of hedging or carrying positions borne by liquidity providers (market makers)

+   Market maker's desired profit spread

−   Discount related to likelihood of offsetting order in a short time frame.

For very liquid ETFs, such as SPY (the SPDR S&P 500), EEM (the iShares MSCI Emerging Markets), or TLT (the iShares 20+ Year Treasury Bond), buyers and sellers are active throughout the trading day. Therefore, because most of these ETF trades are matched extremely quickly and never involve the creation/redemption process, the first three factors do not weigh heavily in their spreads. In high-volume ETFs (e.g., trading more than 1 million shares a day), most orders are easily matched in the electronic order book and market makers have a high likelihood of finding another side or hedging any large orders. These active ETFs have tight bid–ask spreads and trade in the market at small premiums or discounts to their fair values.

For the same reasons, for liquid ETFs that attract large numbers of buyers and sellers, the bid–ask spread can be significantly tighter than those of the underlying securities.

Less actively traded ETFs will have wider bid–ask spreads displayed on quote systems and are commonly traded with the assistance of the ETF desk at a broker/dealer, which will consider the first three factors in making a two-way market.

Note that the longest time a large position needs to be held in a broker/dealer's inventory will be through the end of the trading day because the broker/dealer can create or redeem shares at each day's closing prices for the ETF holdings through the designated AP that transacts with the ETF manager.

Comparing Bid–Ask Spreads and ETF Liquidity

One of the most important drivers of the liquidity and trading costs of an ETF is the market structure and liquidity of the underlying securities or derivatives. For example, fixed-income securities trade in a dealer market and tend to have much wider bid–ask spreads than large-capitalization US stocks. The bid–ask spreads of international ETFs are influenced by whether the market for the underlying securities is open for trading during US market hours. For specialized ETFs—such as those tracking commodities, volatility futures, or even small-cap stocks—bid–ask spreads can be wide simply because the risk of holding a position even for a short period of time can be high. Finally, for some ETFs, even though the underlying securities are liquid, bid–ask spreads may be wide simply because the ETF trades so little that the chances of an AP rolling up enough volume to use the creation/redemption process are low. In those cases, market makers will show a wide spread on the electronic quote screen but the actual spread for a large transaction may be narrower if traders know there is live interest in trading a large quantity of the ETF.

Figure 6.3 shows median bid–ask spreads across various types of ETFs in early 2014. They are median spreads across the universe of US ETFs in each asset class and spanning a wide range of trading volume.

US equity and fixed-income ETFs have the tightest spreads. These ETFs tend to be the most actively traded and also have easily accessible underlying securities that make the ETFs easy to hedge. International equity and fixed-income ETFs have wider bid–offer spreads than ETFs for US equities and fixed income. This difference comes, in part, from the different market structures outside the United States but also exists because underlying securities

Figure 6.3. Median ETF Bid–Ask Spread, as of 31 March 2014

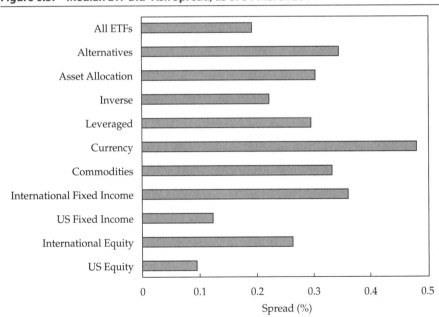

Source: ETF.com.

for many international equity ETFs are difficult to price simultaneously during US trading hours, when some markets are closed, especially in the afternoons. The higher the number of underlying securities that are trading—such as in the morning, when European markets are open—the tighter the spreads will be and the more reliable the prices.

A good way to assess the liquidity and potential trading costs of ETFs is to compare various measures of trading activity among similar funds. **Table 6.2** shows trading measures for some of the most liquid ETFs—SPY and IVV, which are benchmarked to the S&P 500—as well as two benchmarked to the Russell 2000 (IWM and EWRS) and another less active ETF (the iShares MSCI USA Index Fund, EUSA) benchmarked to the MSCI USA Index of large-cap stocks.

SPY is one of the most liquid securities in the world and is much more liquid than IVV. SPY trades almost $19 billion a day on average, compared with

Table 6.2. Large-Cap Equity Index ETF Trading Measures, as of 30 May 2014

ETF	SPY	IVV	EUSA	IWM	EWRS
Benchmark	S&P 500	S&P 500	MSCI USA	Russell 2000	Equal-Weighted Russell 2000
Volume in # of shares					
Daily average volume	102,295,515	2,370,564	55,251	53,482,031	10,319
Median volume	93,561,865	2,912,412	2,062	49,360,448	8,660
Volume in US dollars					
Daily average volume	18.8 billion	615.7 million	2.2 million	6.0 billion	460.4 thousand
Median volume	17.6 billion	555.1 million	82.8 thousand	5.6 billion	372.2 thousand
Other characteristics					
Average spread (%)	0.01	0.01	0.10	0.01	0.29
Average spread ($)	0.01	0.02	0.04	0.01	0.13
Median premium/ discount (%)[a]	0.00	0.01	0.05	0.00	0.05
Maximum premium (%)[a]	0.09	0.10	1.51	0.21	0.59
Maximum discount (%)[a]	−0.25	−0.24	−0.46	−0.39	−0.79

[a]Over previous 12 months.
Source: ETF.com.

$616 million for IVV. A look at the average bid–ask spread shows that both are highly tradable, however, and have tight premiums and discounts to NAV. EUSA, in contrast, has large spreads, even though its holdings overlap the S&P 500 completely. The lower liquidity and higher trading cost for EUSA can also be attributed to the fact that the benchmark index does not have futures and other index products available for use in hedging by market makers.

IWM holds far more securities than the previous three discussed, and many of them are small-cap stocks that, themselves, have wide spreads. It trades with spreads and premiums/discounts nearly as good, however, as SPY. How is that possible? First, trading activity in IWM is ample and ongoing, so the creation/redemption process rarely comes into play. Second, the Russell 2000 that the fund tracks has an active futures market, making it easy for market makers and APs to quickly hedge out the risk of large trades.

EWRS, which holds the same stocks as IWM but in equal weights, has to take much larger positions in the least liquid (smallest) stocks in the Russell 2000, making creation and redemption more expensive for EWRS than for IWM. Furthermore, the nontraditional weighting scheme makes the futures less useful. Finally, because EWRS attracts little investor interest, market makers keep the spreads wide—the average spread as of 30 May 2014 was 0.29%—and the ETF can trade at a significant premium or discount.

When we look outside of equities, understanding spreads becomes trickier. No exchange exists for bonds. Instead, traders at banks and large bond desks quote a bid–ask spread when they receive a trade inquiry, and trades occur with a single counterparty rather than through an exchange. So, although the fixed-income ETFs give investors access to a portfolio of debt securities trading with transparent bid–ask spreads in the stock market, the actual underlying market for those bonds is far less visible.

On the one hand, some bonds, such as US Treasury securities, are actively traded, have tight bid–ask spreads, and even have their bid–ask prices regularly advertised on electronic platforms, such as Bloomberg, where deal bids and offers are aggregated. Corporate debt and high-yield bonds, on the other hand, and even some municipals and international bonds, are actively traded when they are recently issued but then may move into the hands of investors who plan on holding them until maturity. Therefore, bond indexes that contain corporate and high-yield debt focus on smaller subsets of the most liquid high-yield securities. Their bid–ask spreads tend to be wider than ETFs based on stocks or Treasuries because of the risk to the dealer in hedging inventory and also because of the default risk of the securities themselves, especially in periods of weak economic conditions.

Table 6.3 shows three fixed-income ETFs, one Treasury based and two high-yield based. All three are actively traded and have small average bid–ask spreads. JNK and HYG have higher median premiums than TLT, however, which indicates that JNK (the SPDR Barclays High Yield Bond ETF) and HYG (the iShares iBoxx $ High Yield Corporate Bond ETF) have been in a net demand position over most of the 12-month period covered in Table 6.3, so investors have had to typically pay an extra cost above fair value for getting access to a high-yield portfolio via an ETF.

A high median premium also highlights a quirk of the way that NAV is calculated for bond funds. Because bonds do not trade on an exchange, no true "closing prices" are available for valuing the bonds in a portfolio. Instead, ETF issuers rely on bids from bond desks or pricing services to come up with proxy prices. Those prices (being bids) are the "worst-case" value of the bond—the value at which the fund would have to fire-sell it. Thus, all bond funds should be expected to trade at some slight "natural" premium.

Inherent in these comparisons is the notion that the bid–ask spread is not a static number; it varies from moment to moment and can move literally with

Table 6.3. Selected Fixed-Income Index ETF Trading Measures, as of 30 May 2014

ETF	TLT	JNK	HYG
Benchmark	Barclays 20+ Year Treasury	iBoxx Liquid High Yield	Barclays High Yield Liquid
Volume in # of shares			
Daily average volume	7,472,247	3,671,162	3,124,142
Median volume	7,147,736	3,062,776	2,804,361
Volume in US dollars			
Daily average volume	830.8 million	151.5 million	294.6 million
Median volume	779.9 million	126.79 million	264.2 million
Other characteristics			
Average spread (%)	0.01	0.21	0.01
Average spread ($)	0.01	0.01	0.01
Median premium/discount (%)[a]	0.03	0.16	0.25
Maximum premium (%)[a]	0.59	1.16	1.49
Max discount (%)[a]	−0.86	−1.08	−1.13

[a]Last 12 months.
Source: ETF.com.

each trade. The spread tends to widen in volatile market conditions or when information is expected to be released that relates to the underlying index.

Keep in mind when trading ETFs that spreads and liquidity vary throughout the trading day. This intraday trading profile of stocks and ETFs can be mapped by looking at the portion of volume that typically occurs at different intervals throughout the trading day. **Figure 6.4** looks at a single ETF—the iShares Growth ETF, IGV—on a typical trading day in 2012.

As the market opens in Figure 6.4, the ETF, which is liquid, is trading substantially "better" (at a lower cost to the investor) than the average portfolio holding. The reason is simple: Not every stock has a trade at the opening bell; in fact, many might not trade with any real volume for a good half hour. Even IGV, however, has its widest trading spreads of the day at the open. By midmorning, typically the part of the day with the highest volume for the stock market in general, IGV is trading with its narrowest spreads, before gradually settling in to trade around 8 bps wide for the remainder of the day. At the close, the spreads on both the underlying securities and IGV dramatically widen out as market makers pack up for the end of the day.

Note that, during the open and close, assessing the fair value of the ETF is also difficult. After all, if an underlying holding has not traded yet in the day, how do we know how it should be valued in the fair value calculation?

Figure 6.4. IGV Spreads vs. Underlying Stock Spreads: 60-Day Average, as of 16 October 2012

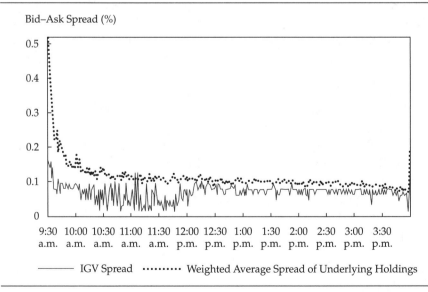

ETF Premiums and Discounts

The discussion of fair value leads to a key concept in ETF pricing—premiums and discounts. An ETF is said to be trading at a premium anytime the last trade was above fair value and at a discount if it traded below fair value.

But what is fair?

At the end of every trading day, every ETF, regardless of structure, publishes its NAV. That NAV is supposed to be a fair and accurate assessment of what one share of that ETF is actually worth. But as we highlighted in the discussion of bonds, compromises often have to be made to set a fair value. Issuers use pricing services to value their bonds. They may choose to use yesterday's closing prices in Tokyo for their Japanese holdings, or they may choose to "fair value" their Japanese holdings—that is, to make a best guess as to their worth—at 4:00 p.m. New York time. If a commodity that is held in the fund stopped trading at 3:00 p.m., the issuer may retain that price at 4:00 p.m. If a fund holds securities in a different currency, it may choose to "strike" the currency at 4:00 p.m. New York time—or occasionally, at 4:00 p.m. London.

Regardless of how the issuer determines price, it publishes that NAV at 4:00 p.m. each day and that price is the official price at which new shares will be issued in exchange for a creation unit from an AP.

During the trading day, all ETFs publish the intraday NAV (INAV), which is also called the "indication of portfolio value" or, in the case of an exchange-traded note, "indicative value." All three versions are supposed to be indications of where an ETF should be trading every 15 seconds throughout the day.

The actual price at which an ETF trades will naturally fluctuate around that intraday NAV. Those times are when we consider a fund to be trading at a premium or discount. At the close, the premium/discount is the closing price relative to NAV. Bid and ask prices can be compared with the INAV prior to the trade to see if the offered bid–ask prices are fair—that is, if the bid–ask midpoint exactly matched the INAV.

For a US equity ETF, the expected premium or discount should be small. After all, US stocks are, in general, liquid, and an AP should leap on any chance to arbitrage mispricing. For securities that are less liquid, however, such as high-yield bonds, premiums and discounts can reflect investor demand.

As shown in **Figure 6.5**, for most of the past few years, HYG has experienced strong inflows. During those inflows, HYG traded at a premium, sometimes as high as 6.6% above fair value. APs simply did not believe they could deliver the underlying bonds efficiently to arbitrage out that premium by creating new shares. Conversely, when the fund experienced outflows in

Figure 6.5. **HYG Premium (Price minus INAV) vs. Net Flows, Daily, 30 March 2009–31 March 2014**

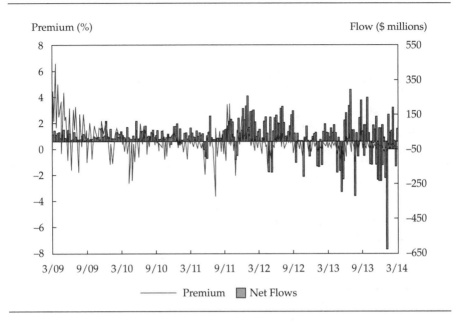

2011, the fund traded at a sharp discount, more than 3.6%. Again, the APs did not believe they could efficiently arbitrage out the discount.

To an investor, all that matters ultimately is the price to be paid and the price to be received. If the investor buys at a discount and sells at a premium, the investor is, effectively, making "free" money on the trade. If the investor buys at a premium and sells at a discount, the investor is leaving money on the table. So, obviously, understanding fair value is important.

Unfortunately, for many ETFs, the INAV is a poor indicator of fair value. INAVs are invariably based on the last traded price of the ETF's underlying holdings. If those last prices are, for example, from the close of the Tokyo market last night, the US-listed ETF tracking Japan will inevitably appear to be at either a premium or discount. But that appearance is a phantom: Premiums or discounts on closed underlying markets are not mispricing; they are, in fact, price discovery. This price discovery happens in illiquid markets, in closed markets, and even in markets with slight time lags (such as the early-closing commodities markets).

Beyond Onscreen Liquidity: Effectively Using ETF Capital Market Desks

The bid–ask spread does not always reflect true on-screen liquidity. Deep and liquid markets can exist even for ETFs with seemingly wide spreads and little secondary market activity. These markets are generally invisible to retail investors, however, and are accessible only to institutions and advisers with the savvy to ferret them out.

Most investment banks have ETF trading desks that make markets and facilitate large trades in ETFs. These trading desks put their own capital to work as market makers. They offset long or short positions in ETFs either through buying and selling the underlying (and perhaps using creation and redemption) or simply by hedging out their risks by using swaps, options, or other derivatives on those underlying securities. Many of these desks focus exclusively on the index-based arbitrage that ETFs have made possible. These desks are called "delta one" desks because they operate with seemingly riskless 1-to-1 hedging of like assets.[15] Even large ETF trades of several hundred million dollars are executed with the assistance of ETF desks at liquidity providers.

Take, for example, an institution or large registered investment adviser that wants to invest $100 million in an ETF representing an emerging market index. The trading desk of the investor may talk to two or three of its typical trading partners on the investment banking side to get a two-sided quote for the trade they wish to execute.

Each trading desk will arrive at a bid–ask price quote based on its cost of hedging, current and anticipated inventory, and the availability of capital to position the trade into its inventory. One or more of these institutions may have an inventory of positions and offer the best possible price. The bank quotes the order to the investors through the salesperson covering the investor, committing to transact at that price. If the investor agrees, the trade is done between the two parties and then reported to the exchange after execution, as in a block trade on a stock. The public transaction record will display the executed price and volume, although the bids and offers never left the telephone lines.

---

[15]In options terminology, "delta" is a measure of the sensitivity of the option price to the underlying security and typically is a decimal between 0 and 1.0 for calls and 0 and –1.0 for puts. (When an option expires in the money, it has a delta of 1 at the expiration point.) Thus, a "delta one" trading desk means all products (portfolios, futures, swaps, or ETFs) have full exposure to the underlying securities.

When looking at the trading activity in some ETFs that are less actively traded, the spikes in activity that occur when trades are facilitated by the capital and hedging ability of a broker/dealer can be visible. Examples of ETFs that can have low average volume but capacity to absorb large trades with low-to-moderate market impact include ETFs based on strategy indexes, such as low-volatility or high-dividend stocks, hedge fund replication, and 130/30 (130% long and 30% short). Such ETFs are often used as alternatives to buy-and-hold mutual funds and are purchased more as strategic rather than tactical holdings. These ETFs may have low levels of average volume and wide quoted bid–ask spreads because they are thinly traded on an ongoing basis. The benchmark indexes are easily hedged by ETF desks, however, because they are composed of actively traded stocks. Institutions can trade them in large blocks with relative ease. Small retail investors may have difficulty doing so.

In summary, because competitive traders are incorporating the risk of making markets and holding ETFs into their full equity trading books, investors can often execute large trades without significantly moving the market price. In addition, APs are always standing by their ETFs to commit capital (like a block trade) because they can create or redeem shares of the ETF at NAV at closing prices each day. It is the liquidity and hedgability of the underlying securities, regardless of the trade size, that sets the limit for the trading costs and liquidity that an ETF buyer or seller will experience.

Other Considerations in Trading ETFs

Other issues that are important for trading ETFs include timing in international markets and market dislocations.

International Timing Issues. Investors who are unaccustomed to dealing with international securities may be surprised to learn that the trading hours of a country can severely affect an ETF's liquidity—even in this age of 24-hour access to everything. In international ETFs, the traditional crutches investors use to evaluate whether an ETF is trading at a fair value—the NAV and the intraday INAV—are rendered largely irrelevant because of time zone issues.

NAV values work well in the United States because the equities that underlie the ETF trade during the same hours as the ETF itself. When the NAV is calculated at 4:00 p.m., or the INAV is calculated intraday, an investor has an apples-to-apples comparison with the fund's trading price. It does not work the same for international equities.

Consider a Chinese equity fund, such as the SPDR S&P China ETF (GXC). Listed in New York, shares of GXC trade all day long and reflect developments in the US equity markets and other factors. The fund stops trading at 4:00 p.m. eastern standard time, when the US exchanges close. That closing price should be the market's best estimation of the fair value of the ETF itself. The fund also calculates its net asset value at 4:00 p.m. eastern standard time. At that point, the actual shares underlying the ETF—which are listed in China—have not traded at all. Naturally, a disconnect occurs between the traded price of the ETF and the price of the underlying securities. Truly, the only thing we can tell by comparing the two numbers is that GXC traded during the day in New York, while China remained closed— which is not necessarily new and needed information.

Figure 6.6, showing a comparison of the price of GXC with its INAV, highlights two aspects of this problem. The INAV tends to trade flat during the US market day, even as the ETF bounces around—which is what we would expect. Indeed, the only movement in the INAV line during the US trading day is the result of currency fluctuations. Note also, however, the trading from 23 January through 26 January, when GXC's INAV stayed placid for three days even as GXC's shares rose sharply. That result is not an error; it reflects the Chinese New Year, when all the underlying securities were closed.

Figure 6.6. GXC Price Discovery: Closing ETF Price vs. INAV, 18 January 2012– 31 January 2012

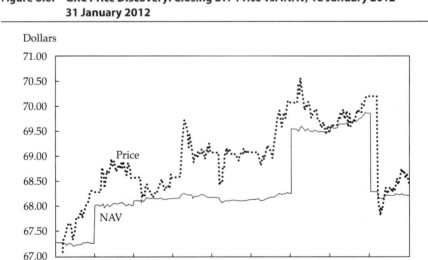

©2015 The CFA Institute Research Foundation

Market Dislocations. Further complications can incur when markets close unexpectedly. For instance, in 2011 during the Arab Spring uprisings, the Egyptian stock market closed but Egyptian stocks trading in London continued to trade. Van Eck had an ETF that provided exposure to Egyptian stocks both on the local exchange and in New York, the Egypt Index ETF (EGPT). When the local exchange closed, Van Eck shut down all creation activity in the fund after receiving a huge influx of cash. After all, Van Eck could not buy stock in the local markets. Despite being closed, investors continued to trade EGPT because it was the best proxy for the underlying Egyptian market while that market was closed. The fund detached massively from its NAV, however, creating the premiums shown in **Figure 6.7**, because the price of many underlying securities froze for a long period of time. Investors, like nature, abhor a vacuum and continued to use EGPT as price discovery.

These kinds of disconnects happen any time an ETF issuer closes a fund for creation/redemption activity, which is more common than one might think. In the past few years, dozens of funds have closed for creations for various reasons, from disruptions in the underlying markets to hitting internal capital limits.

In short, because ETFs trade on the US exchanges just as stocks do, they are subject to any issue that affects those markets. For example, during the 9 May 2010 Flash Crash, which was triggered by large-scale S&P

Figure 6.7. EGPT Premium/Discount, 31 December 2010–29 March 2011

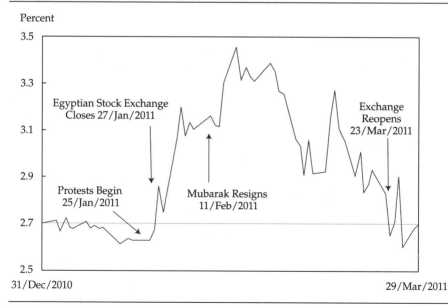

500 futures selling, in which the major stock market indexes collectively fell (and recovered)—some nearly 10% within a few minutes—many ETFs were caught up in the frenzy. Trading in both large-cap and small-cap stocks was chaotic, and it flowed through to ETFs that had these stocks in their indexes. ETF market makers, including many high-frequency trading firms, halted or significantly reduced market-making activities in ETFs. Some of the less liquid ETFs experienced some of the steepest price declines. For some ETF investors unlucky enough to have left "sleeping stop orders"—orders to sell an ETF at the market price should the price ever trade down through a trigger price—losses of more than 20% occurred.

Speculators. Because ETFs can be shorted, they have become a favorite vehicle for some types of speculators. In markets where direct shorting is often difficult (bonds, for instance), ETFs are a highly efficient way of expressing negative sentiment. Of course, shorting comes with its own increased risks, and the costs to borrow in-demand ETFs can soar to astronomical levels during times of market crises. For example, the iShares National AMT-Free Muni Bond ETF (MUB) became a favorite short target during the municipal bond market collapse in the summer of 2013 and cost as much as 10% (annualized) to borrow.

7.   ETF Strategies in Portfolio Management

The liquidity, flexibility, and range of exchange-traded funds and notes make them potential considerations to enhance many portfolio management processes.[16] In any portfolio that relies on index-based exposure, ETFs can be a powerful tool. They can serve as core holdings in virtually every asset class, subasset class, style, sector, country, or thematic strategy and can support tactical or dynamic strategies, portfolio rebalancing, and risk management. They can be tools for passive or active investing and for top-down or bottom-up portfolio construction.

Prior to the availability of ETFs, only the largest institutional investors had easy and low-cost access to many of the investment categories and themes available now in ETFs. As ETFs have grown in size, liquidity, and breadth of coverage, registered investment advisers (RIAs), financial advisers (FAs), and individual investors have used them to explore new dimensions of buy and hold and of dynamic investment strategies. Pension funds, hedge funds, and even institutional asset managers have incorporated ETF strategies into their investment processes.

ETF Products and Strategy Evolution

Even though ETFs are a relatively new product in the financial marketplace, as with most successful investment products, the applications and product offerings have evolved. We can identify three phases in this evolution that correspond to the investment environment in place at the time and natural product extensions building on the success of the prior phases.

Phase 1: Exposure Management and Access for US and Broad International Equity Indexes (1993–2001). In the mid-1990s, US and international equities were posting strong returns with global economic expansion, the boom in technology stocks, and preparation for introduction of the euro. The first ETFs, such as the SPDR S&P 500 Index ETF (SPY) and SPDR S&P MidCap 400 ETF (MDY) together with style and sector indexes from State Street Global Advisers (SSgA), developed an early following among RIAs, individual investors, and hedge funds as easy ways to

---

[16]We use "ETF" through the remainder of this chapter, but all these strategies can be used with ETNs also.

access indexes through a brokerage account. ETFs were also more tax efficient because of the creation/redemption process.

In 2000, Barclays Global Investors launched iShares. As a leading institutional index fund manager, BGI saw an opportunity to introduce individual investors and their financial advisers, who had been pouring money into active mutual funds in the latter half of the 1990s, to global index-based investing via ETFs. With more than 50 offerings, the first batch of iShares included a rebranding of WEBS (World Equity Benchmark Shares) ETFs based on MSCI country indexes and first launched in 1996. The iShares launch also included an array of new ETFs based on US broad-capitalization, style, and sector indexes.

This major expansion of ETF offerings from BGI was a catalyst for Vanguard's eventual entry into the ETF business with VIPERs (Vanguard Index Participation Equity Receipts) in late 2001. As the leading mutual fund index provider, Vanguard did not want to lose current or potential investors to ETF index investing with competitors SSgA or BGI. Vanguard followed a different route, however, by issuing ETFs as special share class of existing mutual funds. So, their large number of index mutual fund investors could elect to convert mutual fund shares easily into ETFs (the reverse—ETFs to mutual fund shares—was not permitted).

In the late 1990s and during the bear market of 2000–2002, hedge funds were looking for ways to hedge technology and other stock holdings and to take short positions. ETFs could be shorted without a plus tick.[17] Moreover, unlike futures, which had to be marked to market daily and held in a separate account, ETFs could be traded like stocks within a hedge fund prime brokerage account. Short positions in the QQQ (NASDAQ 100 Index Tracking Stock) ETF, based on the NASDAQ 100, became a popular means of hedging technology stocks, and other sector index ETFs, together with SPY, were used for tactical trading and hedging purposes.

Phase 2: Indexing in Other Asset Classes and Derivatives in ETFs (2002–2009). In their first decade of availability, ETFs based on equity indexes grew in assets and trading activity but were primarily the province of institutional investors and hedge funds. (And hedge funds were usually

---

[17]Regulations were put in place by the US SEC (Rule 10a-1) in 1938 after the Great Depression to require short sales of ordinary stocks to be executed after a "plus tick" or price rise has taken place. The purpose was to avoid "bear raids"—that is, organized efforts to drive a stock's price down through shorting. This rule was ended in 2007 after studies of its impact by the SEC and a period of public comment. After the financial crisis of 2008, however, an alternative uptick rule regulation was put in place that applied to some stocks after a 10% price decline within a trading day.

using them for short positions.) With the arrival of the three-year equity bear market of 2000–2002, investors sought to expand holdings of fixed income and commodities and to have more ways of making long-term and short-term tactical adjustments to their portfolios. They asked, Why not use ETFs for these purposes?

Index providers, index fund managers, and investment bank ETF desks collaborated to expand ETF products to include established fixed-income and commodity indexes. Investors began to use Barclays Capital (Lehman) bond index ETFs in their fixed-income asset classes and commodity and metals ETFs—based on the iShares S&P GSCI (Goldman Sachs Commodity Index) Commodity Index Trust (GSG) and also on gold via an ETF (SPDR Gold Shares, GLD) backed by a trust that holds gold bullion and that was established by the World Gold Council. GSG and most commodity index ETFs that followed, which were based on rolled positions in a broad set of commodity futures, were quickly adopted by both institutional and individual investors as they looked to diversify into alternatives from stock and bond holdings. ETFs based on currency exposures also became available.

As they began to cover many asset class index categories, ETFs began to be thought of as tools for rebalancing to asset mix targets as well as for tactical overlays. Many pension funds with trading capabilities used both ETFs and swaps for long index exposure, and some RIAs also found a fit for these dynamic allocation tools in their top-down investment strategies.

In 2006, leveraged and inverse ETFs began to become available from ProShares and, later, Direxion, broadening the appeal of using fund-traded products to magnify or reduce risk. These geared (leveraged and inverse) exposures with daily objective target multipliers (such as 2 times, –1 times, or –2 times benchmark returns across a range of asset classes) had been available in mutual fund format since 1993. They were structured as 1940 Act funds with derivative exposures collateralized by US T-bills and cash and came just at the start of a period of general nervousness about a potential bear market in global equity indexes—financial stocks, in particular. Leveraged and inverse ETFs were quickly adopted by institutions, RIAs, broker/dealers, and some sophisticated individual investors for short-term strategies to take bearish or bullish views or to manage risk. With these ETFs, investors could be assured they would not lose more than they invested and could access leveraged or short exposure without the need to open a margin account or have direct positions in derivatives.

As the financial crisis started in 2007 and took root in 2008, investors began to understand the need to expand beyond buy-and-hold investing. Portfolio strategies using ETFs to adjust exposure, manage risk, and expand fixed-income holdings began to grow rapidly in 2008 and beyond as investors sought to change their investment styles after the financial crisis. Many RIAs and FAs began to offer dynamic top-down investment strategies that shifted exposure across asset classes, equity size indexes, or sectors as opportunities and risks in the market changed. These strategies were offered to individual investors for a fee through brokers, insurance companies, and some mutual fund providers. ETFs were the natural implementation vehicles for providers of these strategies, which today we call "ETF managed accounts".

Phase 3: The Rise of "Smart Beta" and Alternative Investment Strategies (2009–2014). The most recent area of growth has been ETFs that are not traditional index funds (i.e., not based on market capitalization). Among these new types of ETFs are rules-based, dynamic, alternative beta, and even active discretionary investment strategies. Many of these ETFs are also known as "smart beta" strategies and are primarily targeted as buy-and-hold investment options. These strategy index ETFs break the traditional index mold by competing to provide attractive return–risk profiles based on their approach to security selection and portfolio construction. They compete with traditional discretionary separate accounts and mutual funds. Because ETFs show representative baskets daily as a basis for creation and redemptions, not all active or discretionary strategies can be adapted to this approach. Many attractive investment approaches, however, that are based on well-diversified and liquid holdings with systematic approaches to investment selection and portfolio building can be packaged as ETFs.

Strategy index ETFs began to be available as early as late 2005 and 2006, but the asset growth has been most dramatic since 2011. The first of these ETFs simply took familiar indexes and reweighted their components on the basis of different factors, such as fundamental factors. In late 2005, PowerShares launched an ETF benchmarked to a Research Affiliates Index (PowerShares FTSE RAFI US 1000, PRF) that weighted stocks on a set of fundamental factors. Soon afterward, WisdomTree launched a host of ETFs covering various segments of the global equity markets but with stocks weighted by dividend payments as a portion of total dividends. In mid-2009, ProShares began to offer an alternative equity beta ETF based on a 130/30 index developed by Andrew Lo of MIT and Pankaj Patel of Credit Suisse.

More recent innovations in strategy indexes have based stock selection on low volatility: In 2011, PowerShares began offering the S&P 500 Low Volatility Portfolio ETF (SPLV), which holds the 100 stocks in the S&P 500 with the lowest volatility. The MSCI USA Minimum Volatility ETF (USMV) from iShares also uses minimum-volatility criteria. All of these

ETFs have seen large inflows in the past two years as investors became open to choosing from ETFs as well as fund products for compelling return opportunities.

Such strategies as global asset allocation and combination strategies that offer some form of risk control are other recent areas of innovation that can fit into the core, tactical, or opportunistic area of the investment portfolio. An example is a WisdomTree ETF, the Japan Hedged Equity Fund (DXJ), which holds a Japan equity index that has currency hedging of the yen to the dollar embedded in the strategy. A recent area of innovation in the form of strategy indexes is offerings from ProShares, MarketVectors, and WisdomTree that have added duration hedging to corporate and high-yield fixed-income indexes. Long bond index exposure is combined with short positions in Treasury futures or Treasury bonds to achieve a duration target of 0.0 with regular rebalancing.

Strategy indexes have also emerged in the area of "liquid alternative" investing. At first, these approaches took the form of ETFs that used rules-based strategies to replicate broad hedge fund indexes (IQ Hedge Multi-Strategy Tracker, QAI, and other ETFs from IndexIQ and ProShares Hedge Replication, HDG). Other strategy indexes offer rules-based, transparent, "hedge fund–like" strategies in specific types of alternatives, such as long–short investing, managed futures, private equity, and merger arbitrage. A successful ETF offered by GlobalX holds, with quarterly rebalancing, the highest-conviction ideas revealed in 13-F filings that hedge funds make with the SEC. Investors can also use ETFs or ETNs to make a bet that the volatility of the stock market will increase or decrease. The relevant ETFs are benchmarked to an index consisting of a rolled strategy position in VIX futures. A "long vol" strategy reduces the risk of equity exposure in sharply falling markets; a "short vol" strategy can be bet that a market will recover from a recent sharp decline.

The most recent generation of ETFs has also seen some successful entrants from traditional active managers, PIMCO being the most prominent. PIMCO's Total Return Active ETF (BOND) was launched in 2012 with an investment objective similar to that of the world's largest mutual fund, the PIMCO Total Return fund. Since its launch, the BOND ETF had grown to more than $3.4 billion in assets in slightly more than a year, as of the end of Q1 2014. Other leading mutual fund companies have filed with the SEC for the ability to offer active ETFs, and we are likely to see much more activity in this area in the coming years. As offerings in these categories grow, investors will probably use ETFs more for buy-and-hold investments, in the form of strategy indexes and active management by portfolio managers who can disclose holdings daily and build successful performance records.

ETF Strategy Roadmap

With the range and diversity of asset classes and fund strategies available in ETFs, they can be found in many segments of the portfolio, aiding many different investment objectives, some with short-term and others with long-term investment horizons. In this section, we explore some of the most common portfolio applications, organized by investment time horizon, to illustrate where and how they fit in fulfilling portfolio functions and objectives.

Exhibit 7.1 provides a roadmap for various ETF uses grouped by their time horizons. Some strategies are related to basic portfolio management functions that use liquid exposures, such as (1) investing cash flows and

Exhibit 7.1. Roadmap for ETF Use in Portfolio Strategies

Strategic: Multiyear Horizon	Both Horizons	Tactical or Horizon < 1 Year
Core index or enhanced index exposure: Use to achieve asset class exposure or enhance strategies based on rules-based indexes.	*Achieve target weight:* Use to rebalance or "complete" set of active investments.	*Invest cash inflows* based on target weights for asset class or category.
Manage strategic investment policy: Use to implement shifts in strategic investment mix; liquidity allows for efficient implementation and, later, funds can be shifted to investment manager or adviser.	*Over- or underweight index exposure:* • Based on investment view • Based on risk objective • As hedge for active stock or fixed-income strategies	*Active or tactical view:* Add or reduce exposure to asset class, country, fixed-income segment, or investment theme.
Asset allocation or "go anywhere" strategy: Strategy to allocate to mix of best-performing top-down investment opportunities relative to risk target.	*Risk factor management*: Modify risk of equity or fixed income (beta or duration).	*Completion strategy:* Fill gaps in asset categories, sectors, or themes.
Strategy index as active or hedge fund manager alternative: Select ETF-based strategy within an asset class or category on the basis of its investment return–risk profile, fees, transparency, or liquidity as the best choice versus a mutual fund or institutional manager.	*Thematic or style tilt investing:* • Dividend tilt • Country exposure with currency hedge • Fixed-income exposure with interest rate hedge	*Portfolio transition:* Hold as interim position during manager or policy shift.

achieving target asset class risk factor weights, (2) investing core holdings as well as overweighting or underweighting index exposure, and (3) risk management. Other strategies packaged in ETFs are evaluated and used like other fund products—based on the attractiveness of their standalone return profiles relative to risk as well as the contribution they make to the overall return and risk of the portfolio.

Strategic Investing with ETFs. Investors have used index and enhanced index exposures in core investment strategies since the first index funds were made available by pioneering asset managers more than 40 years ago. The primary strategic use of ETFs by institutional investors, financial advisers, and individuals is to get simple index exposure in the various asset classes. ETFs make doing so easy—across global equities, bonds, commodities, currencies, and derivatives. ETFs provide the access at lower fees and with more transparency than most other approaches, and they can be traded easily. Because ETFs exist for a broad range of core exposures for virtually all asset classes at competitive fees, many investors use them as an alternative to a mutual fund or a commingled trust fund offered by a money manager.

Asset managers are increasingly using ETFs to implement their top-down investment strategy applications, especially for discretionary asset allocation or global macro strategies. This investment approach when used in equity and fixed-income mutual funds has been called a "go anywhere" or "unconstrained" strategy. ETFs are commonly found in such strategies, which tend to be standalone investment products that allocate to a mix of top-down investment opportunities on the basis of the portfolio manager's expectations of performance. The products are structured to be held over multiyear horizons as a key part of the total portfolio strategy and to provide attractive returns relative to their risk profiles.

Even for positions held for a multiyear horizon, investors from time to time adjust their asset mix as their strategic outlooks change for the expected return and risk of each asset class, as their own risk tolerances change, or simply to maintain a target allocation over time. ETFs are frequently used to execute shifts in asset mixes. Core positions in ETFs are sold in the asset class category taking on a lower weight and new positions acquired in the category taking on a higher target weight. For institutions, the ability to implement the asset mix shift in one buy/sell trade can help minimize the market impact of the shift and make sure the investors are fully invested during the strategic policy change. ETFs are sometimes used in conjunction with separate accounts; the ETF provides the so-called liquidity sleeve in a given asset class allocation.

Increasingly, however, ETFs can be found as the sole investment vehicle in a managed portfolio. Morningstar now tracks ETF managed portfolios, which they define as investment strategies run by investment advisers that have more than 50% of their holdings in ETFs.[18] Morningstar has compiled a database of 151 such managers offering 660 strategies, with combined assets of $103 billion as of the end of March 2014. The managers focused on using ETFs as their primary investment vehicles have seen significant growth in the past few years; assets as of 31 March 2014 climbed some 40% higher than a year prior. According to Morningstar's classification, 52% of the strategies consider global investments in their investment processes whereas others are restricted to US or international markets. These services are typically offered through separately managed accounts available for a fee, either directly through fund wholesalers or on broker/dealer platforms for their financial advisers to use. In addition, many insurance companies offer variable annuities that include "active" asset allocation strategies using ETFs for all or part of the holdings.

Another long-term strategic application of ETFs is to use a "strategy index" ETF or actively managed ETF within an asset class. Here, an investor may view the ETF as the best choice after comparing it with a fund product that uses either actively managed or traditional index strategies and after considering the relative performance, risk profile, fees, transparency, and liquidity of the ETF versus similar competitors. The choices are expanding as ETF managers work with index providers to design innovative strategies that can be specified in terms of a set of rules and packaged in an ETF wrapper. In addition, other mutual fund managers are likely to follow PIMCO and begin to offer ETF versions of their most popular mutual fund products, at least on the part of managers willing to disclose mutual fund holdings or set up a "sibling" fund with a similar investment objective and the same portfolio manager.

Finally, the rise of liquid alternative ETFs has many investors who might have been focused on single-stock portfolios or mutual funds considering ETFs. These funds are often the only liquid means of accessing complex multi-asset or derivatives-based strategies, and they often do so at much lower fees than mutual fund or separate account alternatives. ETFs here are benchmarked to indexes that replicate the performance of hedge funds, long–short equity strategies, and liquid private equity. Other categories available include market-neutral, managed futures, multi-alternative, and volatility-based strategies.[19]

---

[18]Ling-Wei Hew, "ETF Managed Portfolios Landscape Summary, Q1 2014," *Morningstar Fund Research* (9 June 2014).

[19]Joanne Hill, "Active versus Index," *Journal of Indexes*, vol. 16, no. 6 (September/October 2013): 18–29.

ETF Strategies with Both Tactical and Strategic Objectives. Many investors combine index-based and active strategies within a particular asset class. With low fees and high liquidity, ETFs are used for both short-term and long-term horizons to achieve target weights in benchmark exposure. Popular categories are US large-cap, US small-cap, developed non-US market, and emerging market equity exposure. Popular fixed-income categories are investment-grade and high-yield corporate debt. More granular areas in which investors have used ETF exposure include the new categories of bank loans and commodities (including crude oil, gold and other metals, and agricultural products). The ability to transact on exchanges, and in large or small sizes, allows ETFs to be used for rebalancing or entering a new category of investments and holding the position while looking for more active investment opportunities.

Investors may wish to hold an overweighted or underweighted position in a particular investment category or use ETFs for implementation. For example, when the US economy enters a growth phase, some investors may desire to overweight mid-cap stocks as well as corporate and high-yield debt. Because the investor does not know how long the economy will stay in this phase (months or years), the time the position is expected to be held is uncertain, so the ease of entry and exit for positions with ETFs makes them appealing for this approach. The motivation for having a position different from target weights could be based on an investment view or a desire to reduce or increase risk. Another motivation could be that the investor has many active managers in a particular space—for example, small–cap stocks—but wants to be underweighted in small cap as an asset class. An ETF that has inverse exposure to a small-cap index or a short position in an ETF benchmarked to a small-cap index could be used in a "portable alpha" strategy to earn the active small-cap alpha while hedging some of the index exposure.[20]

ETFs are also often used for separately managing exposure to risk factors for both short and long horizons. In this strategy, the investor may have a target factor exposure that is not delivered by the existing asset class allocation. For example, the investor may desire to manage the target equity beta or target bond duration of the entire portfolio. If the target beta or duration differs from the actual beta or duration, an ETF long or short position can provide the desired differential exposure. Other risk factors that investors may want to control could be currency exposure or exposure to a particular

---

[20]Note that if an inverse ETF is used with the objective of earning a target multiplier over a period of more than a few weeks or if it is on a volatile benchmark, the position size should be monitored to see if it needs to be rebalanced to mitigate compounding effects from the daily objective multiplier.

industry, such as energy, financials, or technology.[21] Here, ETFs representing these risk factors can use long, short, leveraged, or inverse strategies to come close to the portfolio goals for major or minor risk factors.

Thematic or style tilting is another strategy that is increasingly implemented with ETFs for both short- and long-term investment horizons. Where once we could categorize investors as being either active or passive, now investors often use such passive products as ETFs to make thematic "bets" that are more often thought of as active. These themes may include strategies based on fundamental or dividend-based stock weighting, quantitative stock selection factors, low-volatility stocks, or even stocks of companies doing buybacks or achieving dividend growth. Fixed-income indexes have also been constructed around securities from debt issuers with high yields or with hedged duration exposures. International investing can be pursued without currency risk by using ETFs that employ currency hedging, and so on.

Tactical ETF Strategies. Tactical strategies using ETFs were among the first ways and continue to be the most common way in which investors use ETFs. The liquidity of ETFs makes them particularly well suited to this purpose. To see which ETFs are used most in tactical strategies, one can look at the ratio of average dollar volume to average assets. Some ETFs—for example, SPY, the iShares MSCI Emerging Markets (EEM), SPDR Dow Jones Industrial Average Trust (DIA), iShares Russell 2000 (IWM), QQQ (the PowerShares QQQ Trust, which tracks the NASDAQ 100), iShares 20+ Year Treasury Bond (TLT), and iShares iBoxx $ Investment Grade Corporate Bond (LQD)—have high volumes relative to assets and are used heavily for short-term and large-scale trading purposes. Many leverage and inverse ETFs on popular bond and stock indexes are also regularly used in tactical strategies; examples include such ETFs as ProShares Ultra (SSO), ProShares UltraShort S&P 500 (SDS), and ProShares UltraShort 20+ Year Treasury (TBT).

One of the first uses of ETFs was actually tactical—cash flow management for funds with equity or fixed-income benchmarks. Many large institutional investors have used ETFs for decades to deal with the relatively small amount of cash flowing in and out of their large funds from dividends or shareholder activity. Investing cash inflows with ETFs allows these investors to stay fully invested quickly and cheaply.

In addition, many financial advisers and institutional investors have allocated a portion of their portfolios for tactical trading on the basis of their outlooks or assessments of current market conditions. This tactical positioning

---

[21]Such a strategy could be useful in pension and individual retirement funds. For example, based on the well-known adage "Do not sell airline stocks to a pilot," the pilot could hold the S&P 500 and a short position in an airline ETF.

can be based on risk factors, country exposure, credit risk or duration risk exposure for fixed income, currencies, or even volatility, crude oil, or metals. Much of this tactical trading is done with ETFs because of their low cost, liquidity, and range of offerings.

Effective portfolio management may also include ETFs for completion strategies where a temporary gap occurs in a particular asset category, sector, or theme. This gap may arise because a manager is being changed or when an existing manager takes an active view that moves the investor out of a segment of the market in which the investor wants to continue to have an exposure. The investor may wish to keep the manager but use a tactical strategy to override the decision for a short period. Another example might be where a group of active managers in a portfolio are all underweighting a particular industry or segment, such as technology or small cap. The investor may not want such a low exposure and can use ETFs to "complete" the desired exposure.

Institutional investors have historically used futures to manage tactical index exposure but have also added ETFs as a key tactical tool. The range of risk exposures available in ETFs is much more diverse and extensive than what is available in the futures market. ETFs include equity style, sector, and industry indexes, as well as fixed-income index exposure. Some institutions prefer to use ETFs rather than futures even for such indexes as the S&P 500 and Russell 2000 for operational or portfolio accounting reasons. ETFs have also gained ground relative to index-based swaps because of the current focus on counterparty risk and on controlling costs and because of the constraints on investment banks in using their balance sheets.

In the past few years, many RIAs have adopted tactical strategies that shift holdings on the basis of models, market outlook, and valuation relative to risk. Also, financial advisers now typically have an allocation of their clients' portfolios that uses ETFs for opportunistic investing. Some do their own selection; others use a model or recommended list of ETFs provided by the ETF research team at their firms.

Transition management refers to the process of keeping target investment allocations in place while hiring and firing managers—or while increasing or reducing funds invested with existing mangers. ETFs are particularly well-suited to this important portfolio function. If a fixed-income manager benchmarked to the Barclay Aggregate Fixed Income Index is terminated, for example, the investor may wish to hold the iShares Core U.S. Aggregate Bond ETF (AGG) while searching for a replacement manager. Institutional managers often "fund" new managers with ETF positions they have held for transition management purposes. The new manager will be provided funds in the form of an ETF position in the benchmark index and then can take time investing in specific security positions that fit the given investment objectives, outlooks, and valuation criteria.

ETF Option Strategies

Options are available and are actively traded on most ETFs representing index exposure and even on some strategy index products. Investors aim to combine both strategic and tactical ETF positions with overwriting strategies using call options; they also use ETF options as a way of achieving asymmetrical participation in the rise or fall of prices by buying put or call options. Selling puts against cash-equivalent positions is a way of buying an ETF at a target price, just as it is with stocks.

The broad availability of options on ETFs has greatly expanded the potential for index-based option strategies on a variety of the index exposures that investors access through ETFs. Essentially all of the option strategies that investors use with S&P 500 options, which are cash-settled index options, can be also executed with SPY or iShares S&P 500 ETF (IVV) options. These ETF options have the advantage of having the underlying ETF for delivery as they would with a stock option and a stock. For example, if an investor has a position in SPY and sells out-of-the-money calls against it that are exercised, she or he can simply deliver the covered SPY position rather than have to sell it to generate the cash as she would with an S&P 500 option.

The active trading of options on ETFs also contributes to the liquidity of ETFs and to ETF assets. ETF and option market makers hedge their positions with a "delta equivalent" ETF exposure. The ability to combine put and call exposures with underlying ETF positions makes ETFs attractive because investors can construct a large set of return profiles with liquid options. Another benefit of options trading is that the market sets a level of expected volatility for the underlying ETF through the implied volatility of the options traded. Therefore, investors can use the information provided by the option market and even express a view on ETF volatility by constructing option strategies that benefit from shifts in the expected volatility of the ETF.

ETFs and Portfolio Management—A Happy Marriage

ETFs have evolved over the past two decades to a point where they serve most of the primary functions of portfolio management—core investing, opportunistic investing, risk management, cash management, and asset allocation. In addition, with lower fees than active mutual funds, more dynamic strategy-based indexes, and tax efficiency, they are giving traditional mutual fund and active institutional managers competition in the performance game. Today, most institutional asset managers and hedge fund managers, as well as RIAs and financial advisers, use ETFs across a wide range of strategies

Not all strategies fit into an ETF wrapper. The disclosure of holdings may be a constraint for less liquid or more concentrated strategies or for more "black box" portfolio managers that cannot be easily described or disclosed without compromising the strategy. The liquidity of the underlying investments must be high enough to handle daily creations and redemptions.

Nevertheless, this road map makes clear that ETFs fit in the choice set for both tactical and strategic investment considerations and are commonly used where a liquid index exposure is a key component of the investment process.

Part II
ETF Asset Classes and Categories

Part I covered the features and key components of the effective use of exchange-traded products in trading and investment strategy: Does the fund deliver on its core promise? Will the market let investors access the pattern of returns represented by that promise? How have investors used ETFs to meet their investment objectives in managing portfolios? These factors are critical considerations for any ETF investor. A question remains, however, for each specific investor: Does the exposure contained in this ETF make sense in the context of *my* portfolio? Even the most efficient, most liquid ETF in the world can be a terrible choice for a given investor if the asset class itself is inappropriate for the intended purpose or if the ETF does not deliver the returns that the investor expects.

Part II contains asset class–specific chapters that dig deeply into these issues. The chapters examine the challenges of indexing and "ETF-wrapping" everything from large-capitalization US equities to commodities and currencies. We cover quantitative concepts, volatility, and inverse and quasi-active strategies. Much of this discussion is relevant regardless of whether the asset class is being accessed through mutual funds, exchange-traded funds or notes, or other pooled investment vehicles. The nuances introduced by the ETF wrapper, however, make the discussions worthy of attention in this guide.

For a handful of ETFs—namely, go-anywhere active strategies, this analysis by asset class will have little relevance. By definition, a true hands-on, managed active fund is much more difficult to analyze than an index or quantitative product. Because holdings can change quickly and unpredictably, any true actively managed product must be assessed individually by using performance attribution and performance analysis, including regression analysis, significance testing, and regime analysis.

Few active managers and active strategies demonstrate long-term out-performance, but ETFs do offer an intriguing package. For an active ETF to pass US SEC hurdles, it must disclose its portfolios daily. This requirement makes active ETFs—perhaps ironically—the most transparent pooled vehicles in the world. This portfolio disclosure is required for authorized participants to do their part in the creation/redemption process. Meanwhile, the benefits of lower costs and greater tax efficiency are retained in active ETFs, which gives them a pronounced advantage over traditional actively managed equity funds.

The challenges of actively managed ETFs are the same as those for any actively managed strategy: The funds tend to be expensive (charging high-management fees), have high turnover (increasing the likelihood of capital gains distributions, even inside the tax-efficient ETF structure), and of course, don't as a rule provide risk-adjusted returns beyond their fees and expenses. ETFs have the additional hurdle of being exchange traded. Because there is no perfect hedge for an actively managed portfolio, APs are hard pressed to keep the extraordinarily tight spreads and tracking of net asset values that are typical of index-based ETFs. Thus, accessing even a proven active manager in an ETF package is difficult.

Even with those caveats, some successful actively managed ETFs exist—notably, the WisdomTree family of currency products and PIMCO's bond ETFs. In both cases, the mandates of the ETFs are narrow, and APs have ample opportunities for hedging in nearby markets.

8. Equity ETFs

More than a quarter of all ETFs are US equity based. They range from broad-based, total market index offerings to ETFs narrowly focused on, for example, only companies involved in supplying wind power. Essentially, if an investor is interested in holding any segment of the equity market, at least one ETF is probably covering it.

This chapter treats US equity ETFs as the base case. Later chapters discuss how other asset classes add nuance and complexity to the decision-making process.

In choosing an equity ETF, the investor should divide the decision into two sets of decisions:

1. How does the ETF *select* the stocks included in the fund?

2. How does the ETF *weight* those stocks once they are on the list?

Starting with the first question, how do funds select their securities? Generally three factors play a role in the selection methodology: size (large, small, etc.), style (growth, value, dividend paying, etc.), and sector (financial companies, transportation companies, etc.).

Size: Capitalization Bands

Although the industry has agreed on how to assess a company's functional market capitalization, index providers must individually decide where to break the list to create small-, mid-, and large-cap subsegments. The debate on where those breaks lie can dramatically affect an ETF's performance.

Academic research supports a clear designation of 70% of cumulative market cap as the large-cap basket. Unfortunately, neither academic research nor the market provides a clear consensus for separating the remainder—the mid-cap and small-cap baskets or, further, the small and micro or large and mega. In dollar values, mid-cap firms in the United States tend to have market capitalizations between $1.5 billion and $10 billion, but the range varies.[22]

Index providers typically set "buffers," so companies do not shift back and forth between capitalization segments as stock prices fluctuate with normal equity market volatility. **Table 8.1** shows the bands for market capitalization for US indexes by index provider.

---

[22]Andrew Clark, "Big and Small: A Statistical Look at Market Capitalization Breakpoints," Thomson Reuters Whitepaper (August 2009): http://is.gd/ieWWsE.

Table 8.1. US Index Market-Cap Bands by Index Family

Index Family/Size	Percentile Range	Buffer
MSCI		
Large cap	Up to 70%	5%
Mid-cap	70–85	±5
Small cap	85–99	±1
FTSE		
Large cap	Up to 68	4
Mid-cap	68–86	6
Small cap	87–97	2
Dow Jones		
Large cap	Up to 70	5
Mid-cap	70–90	±2
Small cap	90–95	–5
Standard & Poor's		
Large cap	Up to 70	±3
Mid-cap	70–85	±3
Small cap	85–100	±3
Wilshire		
Large cap	Up to 85	2.50
Mid-cap	80–90	±2.5
Small cap	85–98	–2.50
Russell		
Large cap	Up to 85	+5
Mid-cap	60–90	–5
Small cap	90+	–5

The buffers cushion the daily fluctuations of a company's stock price and thus its market cap. Some companies are so close to the cutoff point for one categorization or another that these daily movements might cause them to bounce between two categories. The buffer allows a more stable index and reduces unnecessary turnover in the indexes. It is a trade-off with accuracy, however: The larger the buffer, the less specific and less representative the capitalization band.

These distinctions *do* make a difference in fund performance. **Figure 8.1**, **Figure 8.2**, and **Figure 8.3** show, using ETFs as a proxy for size-based indexes from Russell, S&P, and MSCI, the performance of various approaches in the five years to the end of 2012. (We chose this period to exclude Vanguard's index change to FTSE in early 2013.)

The iShares Russell 2000 ETF (IWM) tracks the Russell 2000 Index, which consists of the smallest 2,000 stocks within the Russell 3000 Index. The iShares S&P SmallCap 600 ETF (IJR) tracks the S&P 600 Small-Cap Index, and the Vanguard Small-Cap ETF (VB), in this time period, tracked the MSCI US Small-Cap 1750 Index. As Figure 8.1 shows, differences in the companies included in each small-cap index led to gaps in performance despite overall movement in the same direction. Over the five-year period, IWM was behind, with a cumulative five-year return (not annualized) of only 19.79%. IJR and VB managed more substantial increases, near 30%—a difference of around 10 percentage points. That spread was not constant. Sometimes, it was narrow; sometimes, it was much wider. And of course, it did not always move in a biased way one direction or the other.

Figure 8.1. Cumulative Total Return on US Small-Cap ETFs, 31 December 2007–28 December 2012

Figure 8.2. Cumulative Total Return on US Mid-Cap ETFs, 31 December 2007– 28 December 2012

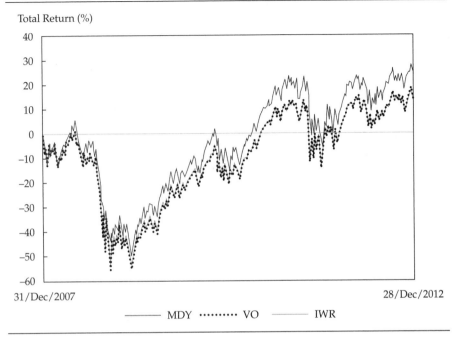

Total Return (%)

31/Dec/2007   28/Dec/2012

———— MDY ·········· VO ———— IWR

Similar differences appear in mid-cap ETFs, as shown in Figure 8.2. The S&P Midcap 400 SPDR (MDY) tracks the S&P 400 Index; the Vanguard Mid-Cap ETF (VO) tracks the MSCI Mid-Cap 450 Index; and the iShares Russell Mid-Cap ETF (IWR) tracks the Russell Mid-Cap Index. Again, the differences are real, with a roughly 10 percentage point total gap (2 points per year) between the lowest-performing funds and the highest. Although the Russell Mid-Cap underperformed in the small-cap space, it outperformed in mid-caps.

As Figure 8.3 shows, for large-cap ETFs, at least in the five years ending 2012, the differences are much less pronounced. The three indexes are, in this case, virtually identical, with a difference of returns between them of less than 1.6 percentage points cumulatively over the five-year stretch. The reason is probably the consensus about what a large-cap company is and the dominance of the largest companies in every large-cap index, regardless of how far down the capitalization spectrum it goes for smaller holdings.

Capitalization-specific indexes do not agree with each other precisely, but the divisions between capitalizations have caught on for good reason. On the one hand, small companies tend to have higher stock volatility, have higher

Figure 8.3. Cumulative Total Return on US Large-Cap ETFs, 31 December 2007– 28 December 2012

Note: SPY is the SPDR S&P 500 Index SPDR ETF; VV is the Vanguard Large-Cap ETF (which tracks the MSCI US Prime Market 750 Index); IWB is the iShares Russell 1000 Index ETF.

risk, and pay lower dividends than large-cap companies. On the other hand, they also may have higher growth potential than their large-cap peers. The merits of segregating by capitalization are supported by the five-year performance chart in **Figure 8.4**. It provides examples of the five-year performance of three SPDR ETFs that track the three capitalization bands using the S&P methodology for the period ending 21 March 2014.

Different investment horizons would, of course, show different results, but clearly segmenting the market into capitalization bands does give investors ways to think about their exposure and use different segments for different investment strategies.

Figure 8.4. Cumulative Total Returns on S&P Large-, Mid-, and Small-Cap Indexes, 31 March 2009–21 March 2014

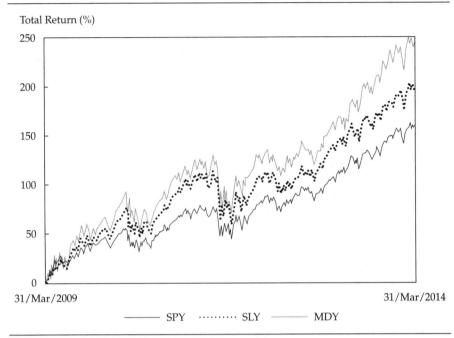

Note: SPY is the large-cap ETF; SLY is the SPDR S&P 600 Small Cap ETF; MDY represents the mid-cap index ETF.

Style: Growth and Value

Market capitalization is often combined with the further style distinction of "growth" versus "value."

Value investing was first popularized in the 1930s by Benjamin Graham and David Dodd, Columbia University professors who believed investors should be buying only stocks that could rationally be determined to be priced below true value. Metrics for undervalued companies commonly include price-to-earnings ratio (P/E), price-to-earnings growth (PEG) ratio, and price-to-book ratio (P/B).

Growth stocks, in contrast, are those that are expected to exceed the average rate of growth for the market. These companies do not typically distribute dividends, trade at higher P/E and P/B metrics, and show strong momentum in their stock prices.

In the 1980s, Morningstar popularized combing these style distinctions with the size component and representing stocks on a grid, as shown in **Figure 8.5.** The market is now well entrenched in describing its products within these bands—small-cap value, large-cap growth, and so on.

For example, both the iShares S&P MidCap 400 Value (IJJ) and the iShares S&P Mid Cap 400 Growth (IJK) follow mid-cap companies, but because of their different styles, they produce very different returns. **Figure 8.6** shows the performance of IJJ and IJK for the five years ending 31 December 2013. In this period, the growth fund outperformed the value fund.

Shifting the time frame to the previous five years, however, as shown in **Figure 8.7,** produces precisely the opposite results.

Although the performance differences between the growth and value styles are pronounced, even within the growth and value categories, there are different definitions and plenty of room for disagreement. What do you do, for instance, with companies that fail to be "growthy" enough or "valuey" enough? Do you keep them out of either index or put them in both? Some systems create a third bucket of "core" equities to fill that niche, thus providing "pure" versions of their growth and value selection lists. Others split the difference, allocating part of the shares of a company on the cusp between value and growth to the value index and the rest of the shares to the growth index. Some simply split the market down the middle.

The industry also has no consensus on what exactly one should measure to divide growth stocks from value stocks. The choice of various accounting, dividend, and momentum factors can yield quite different results.

Figure 8.5. Equity Size and Style Grid

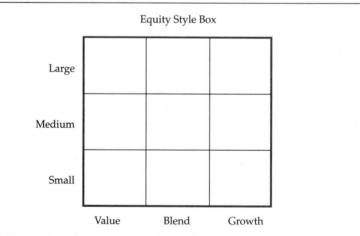

©2015 The CFA Institute Research Foundation

Figure 8.6.   Cumulative Total Returns of S&P Mid-Cap Growth and Mid-Cap Value ETFs, 31 December 2008–31 December 2013

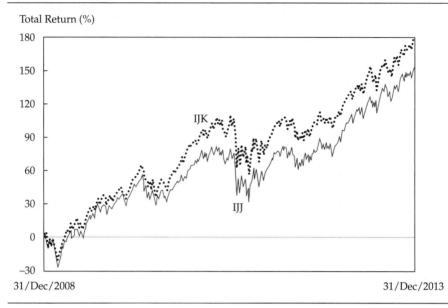

Figure 8.7.   Cumulative Total Returns of S&P Mid-Cap Growth and Mid-Cap Value ETFs, 31 December 2003–30 December 2008

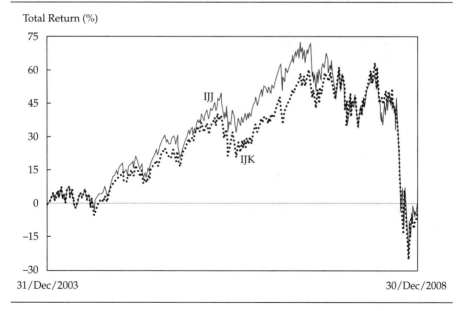

Over the five years and 3 months between 2009 and March 2014 for instance, two ETFs—both purporting to fish for growth stocks out of the S&P 500—have diverged by more than 70 percentage points, as shown in **Figure 8.8**. Clearly, investors making decisions on the growth-to-value spectrum need to have an aggressive opinion about which classification method will perform better in a given market environment.

Figure 8.8. Cumulative Total Return of S&P 500 Growth ETFs, 31 March 2009–31 March 2014

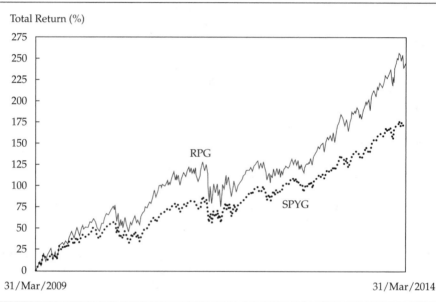

Note: RPG is the Guggenheim S&P 500 Pure Growth ETF; SPYG is the SPDR S&P 500 Growth ETF.

Sector

A third way to select a list of securities for an index is by industry sector. While what constitutes a large-cap or a growth stock is the subject of disagreement among index providers, the distinctions at the sector level can be even more profound.

Classification Systems. Index providers mainly rely on one of two major classification systems—the Global Industry Classification Standard (GICS) and the Industry Classification Benchmark (ICB). Both classification systems are intended to draw useful distinctions between different types of companies.

GICS takes roughly 35,000 companies and divides them into four levels—sectors, industry groups, industries, and subindustries—based on their principal business activity. For its classifications, the system looks at the source of each company's revenues and earnings and also considers prevailing market opinion.

ICB looks at a much larger pool of companies (60,000) but also divides them into four levels—industries, super-sectors, sectors, and subsectors. ICB also assigns companies to buckets based on the primary source of their revenues.

A key difference between these two systems is the universe of companies each system starts with. Starting with a smaller number of companies, as GICS does, may limit the depth available within the sectors.

The next difference can be seen in the top row of **Table 8.2**, where each system divides the companies into sectors or industries. Aside from the confusing nomenclature—a sector is the highest level designation in GICS but the third tier of differentiation in ICB—the systems line up relatively easily at the top. The exception is consumer stocks, where the competing buckets are markedly different at a philosophical level and produce markedly different outcomes for shareholders.

GICS looks at consumer stocks from the standpoint of things consumers can and cannot live without—Consumer Discretionary and Consumer Staples. In this view, demand for the two types of consumer product will vary with the economy—as will those companies' stock performances. Theoretically, companies in the Consumer Discretionary bucket should be more directly tied to the business cycle than Consumer Staples companies.

ICB sorts companies into Consumer Goods or Consumer Services at the top level. The Consumer Goods category contains companies that produce tangible products. The Consumer Services category contains companies that deliver those goods (retailers) and/or provide services and nonphysical goods (e.g., movie studios).

Amazon provides an example of how the classification systems differ. GICS classifies Amazon into its Internet Retailers subindustry, whereas ICB

Table 8.2. Sector Classification Systems Comparison

	GICS		ICB	
Level 1	10	Sectors	10	Industries
Level 2	24	Industry groups	19	Super-sectors
Level 3	68	Industries	41	Sectors
Level 4	154	Subindustries	114	Subsectors

has it in Broadline Retailers. Both classifications seem reasonable, and a case can be made for each. It depends whether you, as an investor, believe Amazon should be in a bucket with eBay or Walmart.

At least three other classification systems exist in the market—Thomson Reuters Business Classification (TRBC), Russell, and Zacks. The systems of both Russell and Zacks are proprietary and are essentially black boxes in terms of construction. Detailed public documentation of their criteria and processes are lacking. No ETFs track indexes based on the TRBC categorization, but ETFs do track indexes based on the Russell and Zacks systems. A number of leveraged and inverse sector ETFs are linked to the Russell 1000 Energy, Financial, and Tech indexes; Zacks is the basis for the Guggenheim Sector Rotation ETF with the ticker XRO.

Classification Systems and Impact on ETF Performance. Let's look at how the differences in classification schemes affect ETF performance using four ETFs following the four buckets of consumer companies in the GICS and ICB classification systems. **Figure 8.9** shows the performance of iShares US Consumer Services ETF (IYC) and US Consumer Goods ETF (IYK), which track ICB-based indexes, and the Consumer Staples Select

Figure 8.9. Cumulative Total Return of S&P Mid-Cap Growth ETFs, 31 December 2007–31 December 2012

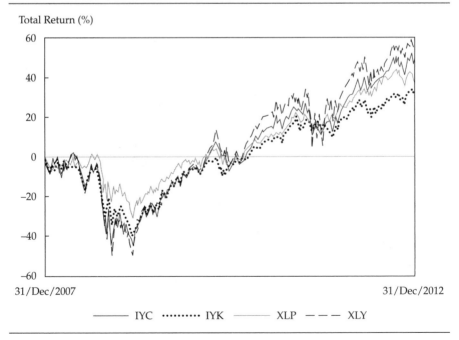

Sector SPDR Fund (XLP) and Consumer Discretionary Select Sector SPDR Fund (XLY), which are State Street ETFs that track GICS-based indexes.

The top two lines represent Consumer Staples and Consumer Goods, and the bottom two lines represent Consumer Discretionary and Consumer Services, which is the correct apples-to-apples comparison of the two naming conventions.

The key goal that sector investors are pursuing is diversification between sectors; they want to see categories as distinct as possible, with performance as widely different as possible. Otherwise, why bother to separate them in the first place? From that standpoint, the effect of these differences is especially well illustrated during periods of high volatility. The GICS-based funds (XLP, XLY), with approximately an 18 percentage point difference in returns during 2008, have diverged more than the ICB-based funds. The two ICB lines—the ones in the middle—differ by only 4.5 percentage points.

Where does that gap come from? Perhaps from the idea previously mentioned that Amazon is classified by GICS in Internet Retailers and thus lives in a different bucket from Walmart. By correctly—at least in this time period—grouping the fast-moving stocks together, real diversification occurs.

Individual company distinctions make an even bigger difference in the smaller universes of stocks—for example, biotechnology. The fewer the companies to choose from, the more the individual classification of each company will matter in the resulting ETF portfolio.

Weighting: How Much to Hold?

The primary mechanism through which most equity ETFs are differentiated is by company coverage in terms of size, style, or sector, but within those categories, further distinctions—and performance differences—arise from differences in weighting schemes. Broadly, the three basic weighting schemes are cap weighting, equal weighting, and "other."

Cap Weighting. In a cap-weighted index or fund, companies are represented according to their footprint in the capital market. The market cap of each company is divided by that of the total market cap of all companies in the selected list, and the securities are held in the index at that percentage.

The theoretical principle behind market-cap weighting is simple: If we want to represent the market, the market has already voted with its dollars. Moreover, a cap-weighted index is the only kind that all investors could hold without any stocks left over. Cap weighting, however, leads to highly top-heavy portfolios. The top 10 holdings of the S&P 500, for instance, account for roughly 20% of the fund. Conversely, more than 300 companies from the smallest holding on up are needed to have the same impact. The relatively tiny weights of the small-cap stocks mean that the performance of the index will be ultimately driven by the largest companies. The smallest holding could double in price, and it would barely show up on the performance statistics for an S&P 500 ETF. In extreme cases—a narrow sector fund, for instance— market-cap weighting can create poorly diversified portfolios, where a few stocks make up the majority of the assets in the index.

One of the great advantages of such a portfolio is that, barring corpo- rate actions that change the float of the companies in the index, market-cap weighting is self-adjusting. As the prices of stocks go up and down in the market, their weights in the portfolio also adjust. The effect is to "let the win- ners run," which some investors like and some do not.

Equal Weighting. An alternative to the perceived problems with cap- italization weighting is to simply hold each security on the selected list in equal weights. For example, in the Rydex S&P Equal Weight ETF (RSP), all 500 components of the S&P 500 ideally have a 0.20% weight. The net effect is to tilt the entire portfolio toward the small-cap end of the list and expose investors to the fate of each company at the same level.

Since market influences change the value of the securities within the ETF, the actual weight of each company is constantly off from the theoreti- cal or target weight of 1/500th of the fund. Thus, equal-weighting strategies need to rebalance back to the target weights, usually quarterly. This necessity increases trading costs and adds the potential for capital gains taxes because the "winners" are the stocks being sold to buy up more of the "losers." Again, for some investors, this strategy of harvesting winners to invest in the los- ers makes intuitive sense, and inside the ETF wrapper, the costs and tax effects of rebalancing are often offset by diligent management of the creation/ redemption process.

Alternative Weighting Schemes. Beyond equal weighting, index pro- viders and fund issuers have begun to offer a range of rules-based weighting and screening methodologies based on company factors, fundamentals, divi- dends, or other features. Dozens of weighting schemes are available—tiered, fundamental, revenue, dividend, and other—all designed to counteract per- ceived flaws of market-cap weighting. These schemes have come to be known as "alternative beta" or even "smart beta" strategies, and each has different performance features relative to market-cap weighting in terms of the market condition in which it outperforms and underperforms.

Alternative beta ETFs have attracted significant assets in recent years. The most widely used alternative beta ETFs are those based on dividend yield and dividend growth, company fundamentals benchmarked to the Fundamental Index methodology pioneered by Research Affiliates, and portfolios built with stocks exhibiting low volatility.[23]

Academic research has not found a persistent advantage of any one weighting scheme over another. Instead, each scheme introduces different factors by which to weight the selected list of securities and introduces predictable value–growth or size tilts. One thing is true, however: Nontraditional weighting schemes introduce additional expense and variability in returns beyond the cost of market-cap weighting, and those costs and risks must be evaluated individually for each ETF.[24]

International Equities

International equities, with 434 US-listed funds and almost a quarter of the total assets under management, are the most popular type of ETF. Investing in international equities can bring with it a bit more complexity, however, than investing in US equities. Currency movements, off-kilter market hours, settlement issues, capital flow restrictions—the further afield you go, the more variables are involved.

Yet, the core decisions about how companies are selected and how that list of securities is weighted remain central to the challenge of investing in both US equities and international equities. Indeed, the primary complication that foreign equities introduce into the classic size/style/sector analysis is the most obvious: country allocations.

Index Selection. Just as index selection plays an important part in the selection of US equity ETFs, it is also important, perhaps even more so, in international equity ETFs. For the most part, each major index provider starts by defining the true universe of investable companies—from the smallest frontier market stock to the largest large-cap stock in the world.

Distinctions between levels of economic development are critical. Take, for example, South Korea. The iShares MSCI Emerging Markets ETF (EEM) follows the MSCI Emerging Markets Index, which defines South

---

[23]For more information on the Research Affiliates methodology, see Robert D. Arnott, Jason Hsu, and Philip Moore, "Fundamental Indexation," *Financial Analysts Journal*, vol. 61, no 2 (February/March 2005): 83–99.

[24]The concept of factor investing and smart beta (the buzzword for alternative weighting) has been the focus of several papers. See, for example, Noel Amenc and Felix Goltz, "Smart Beta 2.0," *Journal of Index Investing*, vol. 4, no. 3 (Winter 2013): 15–23; Jason Hsu, "Value Investing: Smart Beta vs. Style Indexes," *Journal of Index Investing*, vol. 5, no. 1 (Summer 2014): 121–126; Jason Hsu and Vitali Kalesnik, "Finding Smart Beta in the Factor Zoo," Research Affiliates' *Fundamentals* (July 2014); and Luciano Siracusano, "Considering Smart Beta," *Journal of Indexes*, vol. 17, no. 4 (July/August 2014): 44–57.

Korea as an emerging market. EEM devotes more than 16% of its holdings to South Korea, the largest country allocation in the fund. In comparison, the Schwab Emerging Markets Equity ETF (SCHE) follows the FTSE All Emerging Market Index, which designates South Korea as a developed market. Consequently, 0% of that fund is invested there; the result is a big difference for funds theoretically covering the same space.

And consider the size allocation. The smallest listed companies in, say, China, might be larger than the largest listed companies in, say, Chile. So, a large-cap Chilean stock barely makes the grade in relation to Chinese small caps. The investor must decide whether the goal is investing in small caps or simply the broadest definition of emerging markets?

Not surprisingly, the further the investor strays from the United States, the more important the question of access becomes. Finding liquidity in small-cap companies can be challenging, and the investor may encounter restrictions on foreign holdings, investment taxes, and other barriers.

Tracking Error and Difficult Markets. One place the results of the challenges in international investing are visible is in tracking error. As an example, **Figure 8.10** depicts the tracking performance of PEK, the Market Vectors China A-Share ETF. It is one of the few funds trying to track the actual shares trading in mainland China (as opposed to Chinese companies trading in Hong Kong or New York). Because foreign investors are not allowed to hold A-shares, PEK invests in swaps with institutions that can, in turn, directly invest in those A-shares. This creates an enormous tracking problem.

This type of mismatch between a fund and its benchmark creates problems even when the reasons for not owning the underlying securities are less dramatic than in China. Many emerging market ETFs optimize their portfolios by simply not holding the least liquid securities in the index. That optimization always leads to tracking error—positive or negative.

A further—and different—type of optimization can come at the index level itself. When investors want to drill into small or less developed countries, creating *investable* indexes that represent the markets becomes difficult. The registered investment company rules require funds to maintain certain levels of diversification, with minimum numbers of holdings and maximum weighting contributions from certain companies. To get around these issues, some index providers have to create nuanced indexes that use creative means.

A good example is the Vietnam index provided by Market Vectors, which underlies the popular Market Vectors Vietnam ETF (VNM). RIC rules require that no more than 50% of a fund be invested in securities that individually represent more than 5% of the overall portfolio. In markets like

Figure 8.10. Tracking Error in International Equities: PEK vs. Its Benchmark, 1 April 2013–31 March 2014

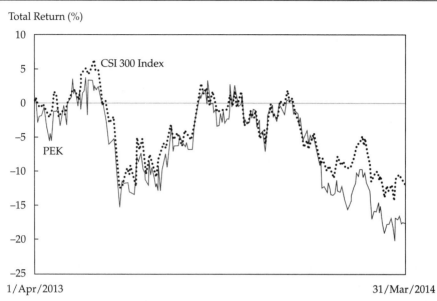

Note: The CSI 300 Index is a cap-weighted index designed to replicate the performance of 300 stocks traded on the Shanghai and Shenzhen stock exchanges.

Vietnam, so few companies are listed on the local exchange that a diversified portfolio is impossible to create. So, to create the Vietnam index, Market Vectors pulled in companies listed on foreign exchanges that do significant business in Vietnam. Although the decision is imperfect from a "pure play" perspective, the result has been to provide believable exposure to Vietnamese securities in a RIC-compliant package.

9. Fixed-Income ETFs

Fixed-income ETFs allow investors to access institutional-level bond portfolios at a scale and cost that were unimaginable at the turn of the 21st century. Because bonds generally trade OTC, ordinary investors incur costly bid–ask spreads when buying small quantities of individual bonds. For decades, bond mutual funds have allowed investors to pool resources and manage bond trading costs, but the funds have been plagued by high fees and underperformance. The advent of fixed-income ETFs has allowed average investors to access a huge range of bond portfolios, most of which are passively managed, thus generally accessible at a reasonable cost. As of March 2014, 228 fixed-income ETFs commanded $264 billion, or 15% of ETF assets in the United States. Some funds are hugely popular, with tens of billions of dollars in assets under management, and some are virtually undiscovered.

Fixed-income funds are nearly as varied as equity funds. They offer control and specificity in geographical exposure, currency exposure, credit quality, maturity, and sector selection. Some funds—such as the iShares Barclays Aggregate Bond ETF (AGG) or the Vanguard Total Bond Market ETF (BND)—offer broad exposure to investment-grade credit, including slices of many sub-asset classes and even some non-US credits. Others focus on a narrow area—for example, emerging Asian local-currency debt, such as the WisdomTree Asia Local Debt ETF (ALD)—or floating-rate senior debt issued by US banks, such as the PowerShares Senior Loan Portfolio (BKLN). Some trade well all day long; others require care when trading. Costs and risk levels vary, as with equity funds.

Understanding ETF Credit Quality

One of the most critical decisions facing fixed-income investors is how much credit risk to take: Do we want the safety of US T-bills or the higher yields of the riskiest junk bonds? Unfortunately, evaluating the credit risk of a bond ETF is not as straightforward as many investors think. Making that evaluation means dealing with two separate issues: (1) assessing the default risk of each portfolio security and (2) figuring out how to roll up those individual risks to a portfolio level. This problem is not limited to ETFs but applies to any bond portfolio.

Most bond ETF investors will rely on the average credit quality of the entire portfolio as reported by the issuer, whose average is based on the bond ratings of one of the major rating agencies, such as Standard & Poor's or Moody's Investors Service. Unfortunately, these ratings seem linear in nature (AAA, AA, A, etc.), whereas the actual risk of each tranche increases exponentially.

Consider a portfolio that has 10 bonds, equally weighted, all maturing on the same date and all paying the same coupons. Nine are rated AAA/Aaa (the highest rating), and one is rated BB+/Ba1 (the 11th rating on this scale).[25] If we use the linear values shown for default probabilities in **Table 9.1**, as

Table 9.1. Credit Default Probability Breakdown

Rating	Linear Value	Five-Year Default Probability
AAA/Aaa	1	0.10%
AA+/Aa1	2	0.10%
AA/Aa2	3	0.20%
AA−/Aa3	4	0.30%
A+/A1	5	0.90%
A/A2	6	0.80%
A−/A3	7	0.80%
BBB+/Baa1	8	1.20%
BBB/Baa2	9	2.00%
BBB−/Baa3	10	3.10%
BB+/Ba1	11	7.30%
BB/Ba2	12	8.10%
BB−/Ba3	13	16.90%
B+/B1	14	20.10%
B/B2	15	25.20%
B−/B3	16	36.90%
CCC+/Caa1	17	47.30%
CCC/Caa2	18	49.90%
CCC−/Caa3	19	67.00%
CC/Ca	20	70.20%
C/C	21	70.20%
Average	11	20.40%
Rating	BB+/Ba1	B+/B1

---

[25]The S&P rating is shown first and then the Moody's rating.

many industry participants do, we will wind up with a weighted average credit quality as follows:

$$\frac{(1 \times 9 \text{ Bonds}) + (11 \times 1 \text{ Bond})}{10} = 2,$$

which maps to AA+/Aa1. If we compute the weighted average probability of default, however, we come up with

$$\frac{(0.1\% \times 9) + (7.3\% \times 1)}{10} = 0.82\%,$$

which maps to a much riskier A/A2 or A–/A3.

Given the disparities in credit assessments and in portfolio-level weighted average credit calculations, investors should look carefully at the credit breakdown for a fund's portfolio to understand the range and central tendencies of the fund's credit exposures. Always keep in mind that each downgrade increases the default risk exponentially.

Understanding Duration and Maturity

Evaluating a fixed-income ETF's maturity and duration is no less daunting than assessing its credit risk. There is no hard-and-fast naming convention for fixed-income funds, at least not a convention that allows an investor to understand a fund's maturity and duration at a glance. Although researchers have found structural differences between large-capitalization and small-/mid-cap equities, no such break occurs along the maturity spectrum. All distinctions between short, intermediate, and long term are arbitrary and not consistent among index providers, fund sponsors, or even sectors. For example, an index provider's definitions of long-term corporate bonds might be any bond with a maturity of 10 years or longer, whereas it might define long-term municipal bonds as starting at a maturity of 22 years. Investors who want to understand the term structure of a bond fund have to examine the portfolio and read the index construction rules to understand what the boundaries are.

To make matters more confusing, even within a set maturity range, ETFs may have different durations, depending on market conditions. Think about the 5- to 10-year maturity range. If issuers (governments or corporations) have been issuing mostly long-term debt in recent years, the fund's weighted average maturity will lean toward the long end and durations will be longer than we might otherwise expect from an intermediate-term fund. A portfolio with a fixed set of rules might well have a time-varying weighted average maturity. What is worse, portfolios that contain callable or mortgage-backed securities will often overstate their average maturities.

Understanding a fund's duration is even trickier. Because calculating a portfolio's duration requires an interest rate model and a set of bond prices, which are hard to come by without access to a bond-pricing service, investors are reliant on fund sponsors' duration estimates. Alas, no industry standard exists for calculating duration—not on inputs and not on calculation methodology. Issuers can and do publish effective duration, modified duration, Macaulay duration, and unadjusted duration, with varying inputs for interest rate shocks. Although issuers publish similar statistics for all their fixed-income funds, one cannot always compare duration estimates for seemingly similar funds from different issuers.

Carefully Considering Currency and Country Risk

Another feature of bond ETFs that is not always straightforward is currency and country risk. Most equities trade in the currency of their issuer's home country. The exceptions generally involve secondary listings and depositary receipts. Not so with fixed income. Companies and some sovereign governments can and often do issue bonds in a variety of currencies. They do this, in many cases, to match income streams in specific currencies.

By convention, bond indexers use the currency of issue to determine a bond's country. Therefore, for example, 5%–10% of the Barclays Capital US Aggregate Bond Index are so-called Yankee bonds, or bonds issued by non-US-based companies in US dollars. At the end of May 2014, this index had exposure to some emerging market and supranational issuers as well as Canadian, British, and German companies.

The currency convention does not hold for emerging market sovereign debt. Some emerging market governments choose to issue US dollar–denominated debt. In this case, the currency of issue does not determine the home country and does not govern index inclusion. Instead, the bond is allocated to the country that issued it. Often, this debt is indexed and accounted for separately from local-currency debt because of the credit risk differential that arises from the inability of the issuers to print US dollars. The investor needs to make sure to choose a fixed-income ETF that provides the desired currency exposure.

Bond ETFs Are Not Bonds

Above and beyond these ETF construction issues, the most critical thing to understand about bond ETFs is that, like bond mutual funds, their behavior differs greatly from that of single bonds. Because portfolios never mature, the only way to value them is by using the market price for each of the bonds held. Thus, bond funds do not offer principal protection in the way that single bonds can: We are not guaranteed to get our money back at a fixed point in the future.

Some ETF issuers have provided a work around for this problem by creating bond portfolios with specific maturity dates—both for corporate bonds and for tax-exempt municipal securities. In exchange for a form of principal protection (barring default, all bonds should pay par at maturity, no matter the price paid for them), investors in these "bullet" maturity funds accept reinvestment risk. These funds pay coupon receipts out to fundholders as dividends each quarter, hold each bond to maturity, and distribute the proceeds to shareholders once all bonds have matured. With these maturing funds, the fundholder becomes responsible for reinvesting the principal and must face whatever market conditions exist at payout time—just like an individual bondholder would.

Illiquidity's Knock-On Effects: Real and Illusory Tracking Error

Bond ETFs have a few problems that their better-known equity counterparts do not. Chief among these are determining the index's level and understanding how that level may differ from the net asset value of a fund that tracks the same index.

This problem has to do with the liquidity in the bond market. On an ordinary day, many bonds do not change hands. Even more bonds trade once or twice during the day, not necessarily within a few minutes of the bond market's close. Therefore, the best way to figure out what a bond is worth on the open market is to use a pricing model. Bond-pricing models take a variety of inputs, including the US Treasury yield curve and pricing, credit ratings, and relative credit assessments for highly liquid bonds. They couple these inputs with information and assumptions about the degrees of similarity and differences of various bonds in the valuation universe to interpolate prices for a whole bond universe.

The issue is that all bond-pricing models require assumptions, so no two will have the same results. When index providers calculate daily returns for a fixed-income index, they rely on these models. They might mitigate the risk of mispricing by using several pricing services and choosing the mean or median value for each bond, but they cannot avoid model risk.

Bond ETF issuers face the same dilemma when calculating their NAVs. The issue, then, is that if they do not use the same pricing service the index providers use or if they treat their data differently, the result will be a disconnect between a bond's NAV and its index. This inadvertent dissonance reflects poorly on the issuer because the fixed-income funds appear to have significant tracking error vis-à-vis their underlying index when no such disconnect exists.

Index-tracking bond funds face the additional challenge of replicating a portfolio that may be illiquid. Since bondholders can get their principal back by holding a bond to maturity, many bonds never trade on the open market after their initial offering. Nonetheless, these bonds exist on corporate balance sheets and in private portfolios; hence, they are included in many indexes. Fixed-income index portfolio managers must do their best to both replicate the returns of the index and manage trading costs. As some equity managers do, fixed-income managers approach this dual task by optimization—that is, choosing a subset of the index's bonds that are designed to mimic the index's exposures (duration, yield to maturity, credit quality, economic sector, currency) well enough to deliver a pattern of returns that closely matches that of the index. Optimizations are never perfect, however, so the investor should expect some divergence, some tracking error, between the returns of the fund and the index it aims to track.

Bond ETFs Providing Price Discovery

Illiquidity in the bond market creates another interesting feature for fixed-income ETFs. Because ETFs are tradable all day long on equity exchanges, they sometimes serve as price discovery vehicles for illiquid asset classes. In the case of fixed income, ETFs can trade when bond markets are closed for the day or are paralyzed. The behavior of LQD (the iShares iBoxx $ Investment Grade Corporate Bond ETF) and HYG (the iShares iBoxx $ High-Yield Corporate ETF) during the Lehman Brothers collapse is a case in point. During the week of 15 September 2008, up to 30% of the bonds in the iBoxx $ Investment Grade Liquid Index never traded. Panic selling was rampant in nearly all asset classes, so the last price was nearly irrelevant for predicting where the market would clear next. At a time when many bond desks could not or would not trade bonds—or widened their spreads to a defensive level— and market participants had no way to value their bond portfolios, LQD and HYG stayed liquid. The trading prices of LQD and HYG became the best real-time estimate of the value of their portfolios and, by extension, of the US investment-grade and high-yield corporate bond markets. These high-profile ETFs became market proxies.

Their prices deviated from their NAVs, but most people assumed that the price was a better indication of their true value than the model-driven NAV calculation.

On a more mundane level is the end-of-day pricing issue for fixed-income ETFs holding US Treasury securities. The US Treasury market closes every day at 3:00 p.m. eastern standard time. Plenty of fixed-income ETFs trade between 3:00 p.m. and 4:00 p.m., when US stock exchanges close. During that hour, the pricing of the ETFs is not strictly tied to their NAVs because the NAVs will be calculated from the last prices of the underlying securities. Late afternoon fixed-income ETF pricing is a raw function of supply and demand and can provide hints as to what bond market participants are thinking the portfolio is worth after hours.

Active Bond Funds

Betting against the market is the raison d'être for actively managed bond funds. As of September 2013, active management in the ETF universe has been most successful in fixed income, with such powerhouse funds as MINT, PIMCO's Enhanced Short Maturity Active Fund; BOND, PIMCO's Total Return Active ETF; and ELD, WisdomTree's Emerging Markets Local Debt Fund—all gathering significant assets. These funds offer the potential to beat their benchmarks. But investors need to be careful. BOND's prospectus offers performance comparisons with the returns of the Barclays Capital US Aggregate without mentioning that BOND can invest in all types of global fixed income. As of October 2013, BOND's fact sheet displayed portfolio holdings of 8% in non-US developed country issuers and 1% in emerging markets. Since BOND's launch, the international and emerging components have sometimes been significant.

As of this writing, actively managed ETFs are required to post their portfolio holdings daily, but this rule could change. Several firms have applied to the US SEC to launch actively managed nontransparent funds (which would follow the same disclosure rules as traditional mutual funds, quarterly reporting with a significant lag). Such ETFs would present challenges for the intraday market-making process, which relies on being able to know how to hedge ETF positions. They would also be more difficult for investors to analyze than those based on transparent indexes. Nevertheless, quarterly disclosure has not impeded the growth of the mutual fund or institutional investment management industry, so down the road we may see ETFs managed by respected active portfolio managers with limited disclosure.

10. Commodity ETFs

ETFs have made investing in commodities cheap and easy for investors of every size and level of sophistication. Before ETFs, if investors wanted to invest in commodities, they had to open up a futures account, get approval from a broker, and maintain margin to cover any movements in the commodities contracts they were holding. Now, those same investors can simply pick an ETF and use their brokerage accounts to buy their chosen amount of exposure.

Investors interested in exposure to commodities, with 112 funds available, have a number of options to choose from. They range from physically backed single-commodity funds, such as the SPDR Gold Shares (GLD), to futures-based commodity baskets. With vast differences between the funds and in the expected patterns of returns, investors would do well to really understand what they are getting into before buying.

What Is in That Commodity ETF?

The two major types of commodity ETFs are (1) those that physically hold a given commodity and (2) those that use futures contracts to gain exposure to a commodity.

Physical commodity ETFs are simple: They store the commodity in a vault somewhere, and each share represents a certain percentage of the stored commodity. Physical commodity ETFs are currently available only for the precious metals—gold, silver, platinum, and palladium—and baskets of them.

Futures-based commodity ETFs are both more prevalent than physical commodity ETFs (by number, if not by assets) and more complicated. These ETFs hold futures contracts linked to the targeted commodity. Futures contracts are agreements to buy the commodity in question at a future date. The contracts are designed to converge with spot returns by the date of their expiration, making them, in theory, good indicators of the underlying commodity's true value. In practice, however, investors often make a basic mistake by assuming that an ETF tied to futures contracts will deliver the spot price of that contract for the duration that it is held. Unfortunately, that assumption does not often hold true.

When an investor buys a futures contract, rarely will the price he or she pays be equivalent to today's spot price. Instead, the investor will pay more or less. As the contracts expire, the manager must sell them and replace them with new ones—a process called "rolling" the position. The simplest ETFs roll their exposure into the nearest-month contract, but ETFs differ in their choice of roll scheme and their location on the curve. And that choice can have a major impact on returns.

The Components of Futures-Based ETF Returns

For a futures-based ETF, the three potential sources of return are the spot yield, the "roll yield," and the cash yield.

Spot price returns are straightforward: They are simply the returns earned as a result of changes in the commodity's spot price based on demand and supply factors for bringing commodities out of inventory and available for current consumption. As mentioned, these returns are the returns that many investors expect to get from commodity ETFs.

For tradable exposure to commodities via rolled futures, the roll yield can be costly for buy-and-hold investors, except in periods when long-term futures prices are lower than short-term futures prices. The issue with investing in commodity futures is that the price of the futures contract may be either more or less than the current spot price; moreover, the price of futures contracts with different expiration dates are subject to contango and backwardation. Contracts are said to be in contango either when the contract an investor currently holds is less expensive than contracts with longer expirations or when that contract comes with a higher price tag than spot. Backwardation is the opposite: An investor's contract is cheaper than spot or more expensive than contracts further out the forward curve. As an example, **Table 10.1** shows the ladder from 31 March 2014 of Henry Hub Natural Gas futures contracts.

When an ETF buys exposure to natural gas, its choice of where to locate on the curve is critical. Suppose the ETF buys the front-month contract in Table 10.1, which is trading at $4.37. At the time of that purchase, suppose spot natural gas is trading at $4.00. We can expect that, as the futures contract approaches expiration, the price of the front-month contract will converge with the spot price. If the spot price stays flat, this position will lose money. If spot climbs from $4.00 to $4.37, the investor will simply stay even.

Most ETFs do not want to hold contracts until expiration because they will be forced to take delivery of the actual commodity and no one wants to deal with 1,000 tanks of liquefied natural gas in their backyard. Therefore, the ETF manager will roll over the position by selling the contract the ETF owns and buying the next month's contract. If, for instance, the ETF sold the front-month contract on 31 March 2014 and bought the next-month contract in Table 10.1, it would be selling natural gas for $4.37 and buying it at $4.40. This act itself does not lose the ETF any money; the ETF simply buys fewer contracts at the higher price. But, again, as the futures contract moves toward expiration, we would expect it to trade down to the spot price (unless the spot price moved up), causing the position to lose value.

In summary, when the out-month contracts are more expensive than the front-month contracts, the market is in contango; when the reverse is true (in

Table 10.1. Natural Gas Futures Contracts, 31 March 2014

Natural Gas Contract Date	Last Price
May 14	$4.37
Jun 14	4.40
Jul 14	4.44
Aug 14	4.44
Sep 14	4.42
Oct 14	4.43
Nov 14	4.48
Dec 14	4.60
Jan 15	4.68
Feb 15	4.64
Mar 15	4.53
Apr 15	4.05

which case investors make money if the spot price stays flat), the market is in backwardation.

The effect can be enormous.

Figure 10.1 shows the real performance of the front-month natural gas index (represented by the US Natural Gas Fund ETF, UNG) versus the performance of the natural gas spot price. In the time period illustrated, the spot price of natural gas broke even but contango caused UNG to plummet by more than 45%.

Of course, the reverse would have happened had natural gas been in backwardation: The ETF investor would have made money in a period when the spot price did not rise.

Note that contango and backwardation are not necessarily persistent; that is, because a commodity happens to be in contango one month does not mean that it will be in the following month. **Table 10.2** shows annualized roll yield costs from different periods for 22 major commodities. Natural gas, for example, had a roll yield cost of 9.45% for the week ending 31 March 2014. At the end of the prior week, the annualized roll yield cost was –1.12%, which would have made a positive contribution to the natural gas ETF returns for that period. Even with these recent swings, the average roll cost over the year ending 31 March 2014 was a minuscule annualized –0.04%, which had a slight positive contribution to rolled natural gas future returns.

Figure 10.1. Effect of Contango on Performance of Natural Gas Futures ETF, 31 March 2011–31 March 2014

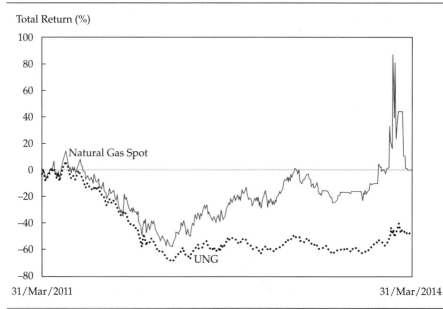

Table 10.2. Comparison of Annualized Roll Yield for Commodities, 31 March 2014

Commodity	Current Week Annualized Roll Yield	Previous Week Annualized Roll Yield	Past Year Average Roll Yield	Five-Year Annualized Roll Yield for 3/31
Energy				
West Texas Intermediate	−8.62%	−8.89%	−0.12%	2.61%
Brent	−1.22%	−2.22%	−0.50%	−0.92%
Henry Hub Natural Gas	9.45%	−1.12%	−0.04%	36.92%
New York Harbor Heating Oil	−2.27%	−0.58%	−0.04%	1.37%
RBOB Gasoline[a]	−5.76%	−2.14%	−0.04%	−8.81%
Precious metals				
Gold	0.14%	−0.05%	0.02%	0.58%
Silver	0.79%	1.02%	0.11%	0.90%
Platinum	0.45%	0.48%	0.17%	0.82%
Palladium	0.36%	0.38%	0.22%	0.70%

(continued)

Table 10.2. Comparison of Annualized Roll Yield for Commodities, 31 March 2014 (continued)

Commodity	Current Week Annualized Roll Yield	Previous Week Annualized Roll Yield	Past Year Average Roll Yield	Five-Year Annualized Roll Yield for 3/31
Base metals				
Copper	−0.90%	0.09%	0.04%	0.50%
Aluminum	8.82%	12.68%	0.84%	7.50%
Zinc	4.34%	2.51%	0.50%	4.41%
Lead	4.16%	6.93%	0.34%	2.28%
Nickel	0.68%	1.43%	0.15%	1.02%
Tin	−0.42%	−0.42%	0.02%	0.57%
Agriculture				
Corn	5.81%	5.64%	−2.45%	3.65%
Wheat	3.71%	1.90%	1.17%	14.09%
Soybeans	−13.33%	−10.74%	−2.97%	−1.69%
Live Cattle	−12.20%	−28.14%	0.14%	1.06%
Lean Hogs	−27.94%	38.06%	0.66%	0.57%
Softs				
Coffee C	7.29%	6.64%	1.67%	8.24%
Cocoa	2.67%	1.85%	0.31%	4.87%
Sugar #11	12.79%	12.97%	1.63%	−9.27%
Cotton #2	0.19%	−5.73%	0.85%	0.42%

[a]RBOB stands for "reformulated gasoline blend-stock for oxygen blending."
Source: Hard Assets Investor, Contango Report (31 March 2014).

In their attempts to minimize the impact of contango and maximize the impact of backwardation, different ETFs have embraced different approaches for deciding where they should be positioned on the futures curve. Some funds track only the front month, but others invest evenly in a strip of contracts covering a year of potential months; still others use a dynamic roll strategy that evaluates each commodity and determines the most profitable place to be on the curve.

All of these strategies carry risk and will perform differently in different markets, and they can have massively different performance. In 2013, for instance, the three main versions of West Texas Intermediate (WTI) crude oil ETF strategies were all up: United States Oil Fund (USO), front-month futures, 10.43%; US 12-Month Oil ETF (USL), 12-month strip, 8.82%; and

PowerShares DB Oil Fund (DBO), an optimized roll strategy, 5.78%. In contrast, in 2012, they were all down: 12.44%, 8.76%, and 9.21%, respectively.

The Challenge of Commodities Indexing

Unlike equities, for which a number of standard benchmark indexes exist that everyone agrees generally represent the market as a whole, there is no consensus on what constitutes a commodity market portfolio. Some indexes are popular, but no equivalent to the S&P 500 Index or Russell 1000 Index is available. Moreover, the two major challenges in creating any benchmark are what to include and what weight to include it at. Although the answers to these challenges are fairly obvious in the United States for a broad equity benchmark—for example, include US-domiciled companies and weight them by market capitalization—the challenges are difficult for commodities.

Consider first the question of which commodities to include. The market has multiple varieties of oil, various types of wheat, and precious metals of various reputations. Should one include platinum or remain with silver alone or gold and silver? Should one include only commodities that trade on US exchanges? Greasy wool is not an important commodity in the United States, but the market for it is big in Australia. Does it make the cut? Moreover, many commodities, such as rice and coal, are not tradable on any exchanges but are certainly important commodities in the world marketplace.

Even after determining which commodities to include, the challenge remains of what is the best way to weight the constituents. There is no market-cap equivalent of something like wheat. Even if it were possible to determine the exact quantity of wheat in existence at a single point in time, the quantity of wheat changes constantly as people eat bread and farmers plant more wheat. Some indexes rely on production weighting systems; others take equal-weighting or cap-weighting approaches. There is no one "answer."

Finally, once the commodities and weights have been decided, which specific contracts should the index hold and how should holdings be rolled forward? For instance, no oil futures contract is the "correct" one. The near-month contract may be the most liquid, but that does not make the next-month contract any less legitimate. The result is shocking disagreement among the major commodity indexes, even at base levels. **Table 10.3** illustrates some of the popular choices.

The differences are simply astounding. Imagine, for comparison, if the S&P 500 had three times the weight in technology that the Russell 1000 had.

As would be expected from indexes with different commodities, weighting schemes, and roll strategies, these major indexes behave differently. **Figure 10.2** shows the performance of various commodity indexes over a five-year period. The cumulative difference between the best-performing and worst-performing segments was 26.19 percentage points.

Table 10.3.   Commodity Index Exposure

Commodity	Deutsche Bank Liquid Commodity Index (DBLCI)	Dow Jones Commodity Index (DJCI)	S&P Goldman Sachs Commodity Index (GSCI)	Continuous Commodity Index (CCI)	Summerhave Dynamic Commodity Index (SDCI)	Rogers International Commodity Index (RICI)
Energy	55.00%	34.34%	69.50%	17.64%	28.57%	44.00%
Agriculture	22.50	33.03	19.60	58.80	42.86	34.90
Precious metals	10.00	17.53	3.90	17.64	7.14	7.10
Base metals	12.50	15.02	7.00	5.88	21.43	14.00

Figure 10.2.   Commodity Index Performance, 31 March 2009–31 March 2014

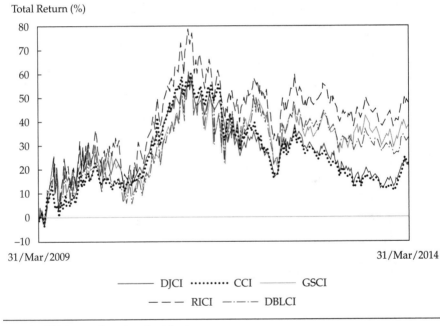

Note: See Table 10.3 for index identifications.

Unfortunately, investors have no simple choice. Whereas equity investors with no particular slant on the market can choose a market-cap-weighted fund and know they are getting "average returns," no such claim can be made for commodities. Investors cannot make an informed choice about which commodity ETF or index to own without at least having a viewpoint on which segment of the commodity space they want to over- or underweight.

11. Currency ETFs

Currency ETFs have done an excellent job of providing access to a market that was difficult for retail investors to access as recently as a decade ago. In the past, an investor needed a separate account to trade currencies and high minimums were involved. Today, an individual investor can gain exposure to, say, the Swiss franc with less than $100 and a brokerage account.

As with other niche asset classes, however, currency ETFs have quirks that need to be considered.

Currency ETFs: Overview

Since the first currency ETF was launched in 2005, the sector has grown to include 24 currency funds, which hold $1.87 billion in assets under management—$3.47 billion if leveraged and inverse funds are included. **Table 11.1** summarizes the single-currency ETFs available in the US market as of the end of March 2014. Within those funds, there are nine single-currency funds covering 10 different currencies, six basket currency funds, and a number of leveraged and inverse products.

Table 11.1. Summary of US-Listed Currency ETFs, as of 31 March 2014

Single-Currency Funds		Basket Currency Funds		Inverse/Leverage Currency Funds	
Currency	No.	Basket	No.	Fund	No.
Australian dollar	1	Emerging markets	4	US dollar index 3X (inverse basket)	1
Brazilian real	1	Short US dollar index (long basket)	1	US dollar index (inverse basket)	1
Canadian dollar	1	Commodity currencies	1	Inverse euro 2X	2
Chinese renminbi	3	Global currency strategy	1	Inverse Japanese yen 2X	1
Euro	2			Inverse US dollar index 3X (long basket)	1
Indian rupee	2			Inverse Australian dollar 2X	1
Japanese yen	2			Leveraged euro	2
Pound sterling	2			Leveraged Japanese yen	1
Swedish krona	1			Leveraged Australian dollar 2X	1
Swiss franc	1				

Source: ETF.com.

©2015 The CFA Institute Research Foundation

Currency ETFs: Structure

Structure determines much that is important about currency ETFs: taxes, investment and credit risks, and payoffs. The currency ETF market currently has four main structures—exchange-traded notes, open-end funds, grantor trusts, and limited partnerships.

Currency ETNs. The first exchange-traded currency products were actually exchange-traded notes, partly because notes are simple in structure and easy for issuers to launch under the regulatory structure for company debt. Remember, an ETN is simply debt—a structured note that promises to pay out returns based on a specific index. Currency ETNs promise to pay out an amount based on the spot exchange rate of the currency relative to the dollar on a specific date. The currency is "invested" at the overnight interest rate. Income from this imputed interest is embedded back into the value of the note.

The advantage of a currency ETN is that it provides access to parts of the market that were difficult to access through traditional fund structures. The caveat for investors is counterparty risk: The entire value of the note depends on the credit of the underwriter.

Moreover, remember that, although these notes do not actually send investors a check, taxes are still owed on the embedded gains at ordinary income tax rates each year. Any further gain realized on the sale of the ETN will also be taxed at ordinary income rates. (Chapter 4 provides information on taxation.) This characteristic makes currency ETNs particularly unsuitable for taxable accounts.

Currency Grantor Trusts (Securities Act of 1933). Grantor trusts are governed by the 1933 Act. The trust holds currency in foreign bank deposits, which accrue an overnight rate of interest that is paid out monthly. Think of grantor trusts in the currency ETF space as equitized, shared bank accounts. As such, they entail an element of counterparty risk because the fund's deposits are not insured by a financial authority, such as the Federal Deposit Insurance Corporation, and, theoretically, investors would have to wait in line with other debtors should the bank become insolvent.

Monthly distributions are taxed at ordinary income tax rates, and any gain on the sale of ETF shares is also taxed at ordinary income tax rates.

Currency Open-End Funds (Investment Company Act of 1940). Currency funds organized as open-end funds under the 1940 Act gain their exposure to currency in non-deliverable forward agreements that are collateralized by short-term investments, such as T-bills, money market investments, and the like. These funds entail an element of active management because the fund manager can choose the term structure of the contracts as far as nine months out.

Gains from distributions arising from the contracts receive 60%/40% (or "60/40") treatment; 60% of the gains from distributions are taxed at long-term rates, and 40% of the gains from distributions are taxed at short-term rates. Distributions from the short-term securities are liable to be taxed at ordinary income rates.

Any gain arising from the sale of ETF shares gets regular short-term/long-term treatment like a plain-vanilla equity ETF.

Currency Limited Partnerships (Securities Act of 1933). Limited partnerships are organized under the 1933 Act and can be used for single-currency funds, basket funds, and leveraged funds. LPs can hold a wide range of securities—futures, swaps, options, and forward agreements—to gain currency exposures.

Gains from distributions and the sale of ETF shares are taxed at a 60/40 rate.

The China Problem. Most currency ETF decisions simply involve the structure, but China presents a special problem. Because the renminbi is not freely tradable, ETFs tracking it are forced to rely on non-deliverable forward contracts. Three funds are in this situation—the Market Vectors Chinese Renminbi ETN (CNY), the WisdomTree Dreyfus Chinese Yuan Strategy Fund (CYB), and the CurrencyShares Chinese Renminbi ETF (FXCH).

Figure 11.1 shows a plot of CNY and CYB against the spot price of the renminbi (as represented by the CNY/USD cross; note the CurrencyShares product is a recent launch, so it is not included in the figure). Both CYB and CNY reveal some difficulty in tracking the spot price because, for the most part, China has kept its currency market closed to foreigners and these products use forward contracts to gain exposure to the currency price movements.

In the summer of 2010, the Chinese government switched to a floating exchange rate—a move that loosened the currency market—and the renminbi steadily climbed. (The renminbi floats against a reference basket of currency securities.) As Figure 11.1 shows, the two products reacted differently when this happened. CYB was in long-term non-deliverable forward contracts and benefited from the sudden rally in the spot currency price. CNY was tracking an index that used three-month forward contracts. These contracts were in contango, which sapped CNY's returns. Here we have two funds supposedly tracking the same thing, but because of the strategy they used to gain exposure, they brought investors completely different returns.

Figure 11.1. **The Chinese Currency Problem: Differential Returns on Renminbi ETFs, 31 December 2009–31 December 2012**

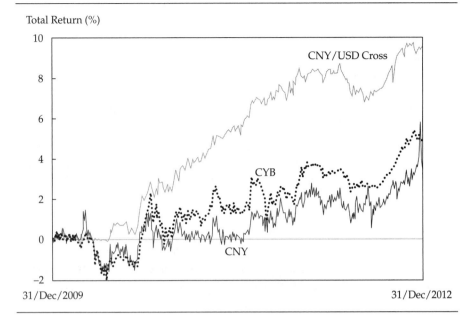

12.   Alternatives ETFs

One of the most interesting areas of the ETF market is so-called alternatives. But what exactly is an alternatives exchange-traded fund?

Roughly 40 funds occupy the alternative ETF space, and they provide two broad categories of product: absolute return funds and tactical funds giving access to unique patterns of returns, such as volatility-focused products. (We use the term "absolute return" here to mean strategies with an objective of delivering attractive performance relative to downside risk and without a traditional security-based benchmark. Therefore, absolute return strategies would also apply to most hedge fund structures.) As of early 2014, 29 absolute return ETF products and 13 of the more tactical funds, excluding leveraged and inverse funds, were operating. **Table 12.1** breaks down these alternative ETFs by type of strategy.

Why do investors consider alternatives? Alternatives are used for two primary objectives. First, they can be used to reduce volatility and manage risk in investment portfolios. They can provide diversification to reduce overall portfolio risk or to help hedge against declines in equities or bonds. Second, they can enhance returns by investing in unique asset classes. A given alternatives

Table 12.1.   Absolute Return and Tactical Alternative ETFs, as of 31 March 2014

Absolute Returns	No.	Tactical Tools	No.
Global Macro		*Spreads*	
Hedge fund replication	2	Inflation	2
Inflation	3	Long–short volatility	1
Low correlation	1	Risk	1
Tactical asset allocation	3	Yield curve	1
Trend following	1		
Long–Short		*Volatility*	
Long–short broad based	4	S&P 500 Index mid-term	4
Long–short commodities	1	S&P 500 short term	3
Long–short currency	2	Trend following	1
Long–short equity	9		
Merger arbitrage	3		

Note: Leveraged and inverse funds are excluded.
Source: ETF.com.

©2015 The CFA Institute Research Foundation

fund may have features similar to asset classes the investor wants to access, such as commodities, currencies, and volatility. They can also be dynamic investment strategies based on rules or discretionary management that have an absolute return objective. In this case, the objective is to maximize returns relative to a given risk level, with the goal of limiting downside risk rather than beating a particular benchmark. These alternative strategies typically use complex investment techniques, such as leverage and shorting with implementation via derivatives.

Historically, alternative strategies have been accessed through hedge funds, funds of hedge funds, commodity trading advisers, or direct investment via listed or OTC derivatives. In all cases, except listed derivatives, these methods of access have limited liquidity; most hedge funds and funds of funds offer access to funds once a quarter, with a notice period for withdrawals. In the past few years, alternatives have become more broadly available in mutual funds as well as in exchange-traded funds and notes. The term "liquid alternatives" has been used to refer to alternative investments that can accept inflows and outflows at least once a day.

History and Growth of Liquid Alternative Strategies

Alternative strategies have been used for decades by institutional investors, led by the largest endowments and foundations, as high exposures to equity risk after the 1970s bear market devastated their investment portfolios and spending budgets. Pension funds became converts to alternatives after a similar experience in the 2000–02 equity bear market, when they found their funded status eroded because of their high commitments (60%–70%) to equity exposure.

The largest categories of alternatives for institutions have been hedge funds and private equity strategies, which are typically set up as separate categories of the asset mix, often with the assistance of consultants in the manager selection process. Funds of funds have been used by investors that needed or desired to outsource the selection, risk management, and monitoring process. Recent defined-benefit pension fund data show that private equity and other alternatives make up 16% of corporate plan assets and 14% of public pension fund holdings.[26] The largest endowments reporting to the National Association of College and University Business Officers (NACUBO) annual

---

[26]"P&I's Top 1,000 Largest Pension Plans," *Pension & Investments* (4 February 2013). Asset data are as of 30 September 2013.

survey have considerable allocations to alternatives; those with assets greater than $1 billion have a 61% weight in alternatives.[27]

With the rising adoption of alternatives has come the reluctant acceptance on the part of institutional investors of the idea that these investments are less liquid and less transparent than traditional asset-manager products and have higher fees. The supply of assets in the alternatives space has been such that favored managers can set their terms, such as quarterly access to invest or withdraw funds, notice periods, limited visibility into positions, and performance-related fees. These terms and capacity constraints have limited asset managers' abilities to offer alternative strategies used by institutions in mutual fund or ETF form. Thus, access is closed to most individual investors, financial advisers, and all but the largest registered investment advisers.

Conditions changed for the alternatives managers after the extremely challenging equity market environment of 2007 through early 2009. The growth of institutional interest slowed a bit as many hedge funds and funds of funds delivered downside performance worse than investors had expected. Moreover, the lack of liquidity in these strategies became a bigger drawback than anticipated for investors who wanted to reduce risk and raise cash.

Following the 2007–09 financial crisis, individual investors looked for investment opportunities that offered attractive performance with low downside risk and diversification away from equities and bonds. The mutual fund industry, seeing outflows from many of its largest equity products, reconfigured existing strategies into products that had absolute return benchmarks, typically US T-bill yields plus a risk premium (depending on the nature of the strategy). Global macro, long–short, market-neutral, and multi-alternative offerings and new funds in categories, such as event-driven or fixed-income relative value strategies, were added to the product mixes. In some cases, mutual funds made the additions by developing subadviser relationships with experienced alternatives managers. Many of the large asset managers that serviced both institutional and individual investors modified their institutional products and repackaged them to fit the mutual fund regulatory framework.

After 10 years of low equity returns and two bear markets, investors at the end of the 2010s also became open to accessing a broader range of asset classes and risk management strategies to diversify the high-risk contribution of equities in their portfolios. Futures on the Chicago Board Options Exchange Volatility Index are one way in which investors have tried to hedge their equity risk. VIX futures have also been the basis for a successful

---

[27]On a dollar-weighted basis, the alternative weight is 54% across all endowments. It is 28% on an equal-weighted basis (from the 2012 NACUBO–Common Fund Study of Endowments Asset Allocation).

category of "volatility exposure" ETFs and ETNs; the category had assets of $1.4 billion (excluding leveraged and inverse funds) as of 31 March 2014. These products are benchmarked to VIX futures indexes or dynamic strategies based on these indexes that derive their returns from changes in expected S&P 500 Index volatility as reflected in VIX futures prices and from the cost or benefit of rolling VIX futures to maintain the characteristics of the index. These indexes and ETFs are similar in construction to those based on commodity futures, but the VIX futures products roll a constant percentage every day to maintain a fixed window of expected VIX exposure (e.g., one month or five months into the future).

Evaluating Absolute Return ETFs

The 29 ETFs that follow absolute return strategies as of Q1 2014, as shown in **Table 12.2**, are broadly similar in one regard: They use strategies more familiar to hedge fund investors than to traditional mutual fund investors. Perhaps more than in any category of ETFs, each individual strategy needs to be evaluated individually and at the prospectus level. Each of the ETFs in Table 12.2 makes a claim to provide a given pattern of returns by using a unique strategy—from long–short equities to hedge fund replication with quantitative models to managed futures.

Table 12.2.   Absolute Return Strategy ETFs, 31 March 2014

Ticker	Name	Assets under Management ($ millions)	Expense Ratio	Strategy
QAI	IQ Hedge Multi-Strategy Tracker	696.29	0.94%	Hedge fund replication
DBV	PowerShares DB G10 Currency Harvest	177.73	0.81	Long–short currency
WDTI	WisdomTree Managed Futures Strategy	147.67	0.96	Long–short broad based
RLY	SPDR SSgA Multi-Asset Real Return	118.16	0.70	Inflation
CSMA	Credit Suisse Merger Arbitrage Liquid ETN	52.01	1.05	Merger arbitrage
RALS	ProShares RAFI Long–Short	49.28	0.95	Long–short equity
GTAA	AdviserShares Cambria Global Tactical	36.92	1.59	Trend following
HDG	ProShares Hedge Replication	35.45	0.95	Hedge fund replication

(continued)

Table 12.2.   Absolute Return Strategy ETFs, 31 March 2014 (continued)

Ticker	Name	Assets under Management ($ millions)	Expense Ratio	Strategy
AGLS	AdviserShares Accuvest Global Long Short	31.25	4.28%	Long–short equity
MNA	IQ Merger Arbitrage	29.87	0.77	Merger arbitrage
LSC	ELEMENTS S&P Commodity Trends Indicator - Total Return ETN	28.56	0.75	Long–short commodities
VEGA	AdviserShares STAR Global Buy-Write	26.68	2.10	Tactical asset allocation
MCRO	IQ Hedge Macro Tracker	26.54	1.00	Tactical asset allocation
CPI	IQ Real Return	26.24	0.68	Inflation
MATH	AdviserShares Meidell Tactical Advantage	16.82	1.63	Tactical asset allocation
QMN	IQ Hedge Market Neutral Tracker	16.68	0.99	Long–short broad based
CSLS	Credit Suisse Long–Short Liquid ETN	13.20	0.95	Long–short equity
GIVE	AdviserShares Global Echo	9.09	1.61	Low correlation
QEH	AdviserShares QAM Equity Hedge	8.39	1.64	Long–short equity
ICI	iPath Optimized Currency Carry ETN	7.85	0.65	Long–short currency
FMF	First Trust Morningstar Managed Futures Strategy	5.07	0.95	Long–short broad based
RRF	WisdomTree Global Real Return	4.58	0.61	Inflation
MRGR	ProShares Merger	3.73	0.75	Merger arbitrage
BTAL	QuantShares U.S. Market Neutral Anti-Beta	2.88	3.22	Long–short equity
CSMN	Credit Suisse Market Neutral Equity ETN	2.51	1.05	Long–short equity
CHEP	QuantShares U.S. Market Neutral Value	1.39	3.05	Long–short equity
SIZ	QuantShares U.S. Market Neutral Size	1.30	3.81	Long–short equity
MOM	QuantShares U.S. Market Neutral Momentum	1.27	3.73	Long–short equity
GLDE	AdviserShares International Gold	1.27	1.52	Broad based

Note: Leveraged and inverse volatility ETFs and ETNs are excluded.
Source: ETF.com.

One thing that these ETFs do have in common is expenses. None of the competitors in the alternatives space are cheap when compared with other indexes packaged in ETFs—especially considering the "all-in costs," which are not only management fees but also any acquired fund fees for owning other ETFs or business development companies, and any dividends owed on short positions. Trading costs may also be high when compared with those of simple index-tracking ETFs. These liquid alternatives are significantly cheaper, however, than liquid alternative mutual funds, which have fees, on average, about twice as high as those packaged in ETFs.[28]

Volatility Exposure and Other Tactical ETFs

None of the absolute return products has come close to the popularity of volatility-based products in the tactical tool segment. This segment, shown in **Table 12.3**, contains 13 funds (this number would be 28 if leveraged and inverse funds were included). Although the mix contains some interesting (and expensive) niche products, they all pale in comparison with the asset size of the volatility products, which are the only products in this segment to have attracted more than token interest. Still, the other funds in the segment—those promising unique exposures, such as direct exposure to only the contango of given commodities or the spreads between Treasury Inflation-Protected Securities and US Treasuries—are worth noting for their potential use in special portfolio situations.

Currently, the most accessible and well-known measure of stock market volatility is the VIX. This index and its earlier form, the VXO, has a history going back to 1986, as shown in **Figure 12.1**. It is a measure of market expectations for near-term (over the next 30 days) volatility derived from liquid S&P 500 option prices. As Figure 12.1 shows, expectations of volatility, as represented by VIX, move with but are different from realized volatility, which tends to be somewhat lower than expected volatility, except when both are at levels well above normal.

Investors focus on the VIX because it has the salutary quality of tending to move in the opposite direction of the S&P 500, especially during periods of steep declines in equity prices. The VIX itself is enormously volatile, however, with a standard deviation more than five times that of the S&P 500 (often more than 100% annualized).

---

[28]Joanne Hill, "Active versus Index."

Table 12.3.   Tactical Tool ETFs, 31 March 2014

Ticker	Name	Assets under Management ($ millions)	Expense Ratio	Strategy	Niche
VXX	iPath S&P 500 VIX Short-Term Futures ETN	1,106.12	0.89%	Volatility	S&P 500 short-term
VIXY	ProShares VIX Short-Term	117.73	0.83	Volatility	S&P 500 short-term
VXZ	iPath S&P 500 VIX Mid-Term Futures ETN	80.51	0.89	Volatility	S&P 500 mid-term
VIXM	ProShares VIX Mid-Term	57.79	0.83	Volatility	S&P 500 mid-term
XVZ	iPath S&P Dynamic VIX ETN	44.01	0.95	Volatility	Trend following
STPP	iPath U.S. Treasury Steepener ETN	19.81	0.99	Spreads	Yield curve
XVIX	ETRACS Daily Long-Short VIX ETN	12.60	0.85	Spreads	Long–short volatility
ONN	ETRACS Fisher-Gartman Risk On ETN	11.93	0.85	Spreads	Risk
VIIX	VelocityShares VIX Short Term ETN	9.60	0.89	Volatility	S&P 500 short-term
INFL	PowerShares DB US Inflation ETN	3.60	0.75	Spreads	Inflation
RINF	ProShares 30 Year TIPS/TSY Spread	3.56	0.75	Spreads	Inflation
CVOL	C-Tracks Citi Volatility ETN	3.25	1.15	Volatility	S&P 500 mid-term
VIIZ	VelocityShares VIX Mid-Term ETN	1.89	0.89	Volatility	S&P 500 mid-term

Note: Leveraged and inverse volatility EFTs and ETNs are excluded.
Source: ETF.com.

Figure 12.1. S&P 500 30-Day Rolling Realized Volatility and the VIX vs. S&P 500, 1986–2013

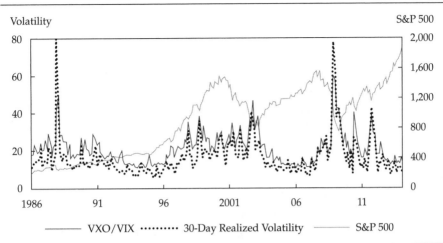

Note: The VXO was used for January 1986–September 2003; the VIX was used for September 2003–December 2013.
Source: Bloomberg (December 2013).

The VIX, although widely followed, is not tradable because of the extent to which its component near-term S&P 500 options shift in weight and properties from day to day. Instead, tradable volatility exposure is available in the form of VIX futures and options, which reflect the market's expectations for the VIX at different points in the future, with expirations out to nine months. VIX futures began trading in 2004 and have grown rapidly in both volume and open interest since 2009 in concert with the growth of VIX futures ETFs. In Q3 2013, average daily futures volume was 148,000 contracts and open interest was 409,146 contracts. The CBOE has also introduced futures based on VIX-type indexes calculated from index options on the Russell 2000 Index, emerging markets (proxied by the iShares Emerging Markets ETF, EEM), the NASDAQ 100, and the SPDR Gold Trust (GLD), but exchange-traded products have yet to be launched on these other VIX-family futures.

Exchange-traded products focused on volatility tend to track indexes of these VIX futures, with various tweaks (long or short, front month, or with differing roll strategies). As with all alternative ETFs, none of them are exactly cheap, but they do provide tactical tools for investors looking to express an opinion about market volatility.

VIX Futures Pricing Patterns: Contango and Backwardation

One warning about the rise of volatility-tracking ETFs is that, precisely as in commodities, the VIX futures tracked by the ETFs are not, in fact, the VIX spot price itself. And in the same way that commodity ETFs have to wrestle with contango and backwardation, so also do VIX futures–based products.

When looking at the behavior of implied volatility, the VIX and VIX futures, a helpful approach is to recognize that implied index volatility has properties similar to bond yields, in that they both have a term structure of pricing that is generally upward sloping. Bonds tend to have higher yields the longer their maturity, and VIX futures tend to have higher prices for longer expirations. This futures price pattern, which is the contango pattern, is the dominant VIX futures term structure pattern in periods of low or even normal volatility levels for the S&P 500 (about 75% of the time). The main reason is that when investors form their views of implied volatility for long periods, they incorporate the chance that markets could shift quickly into a high-volatility regime with a surge in the VIX to levels that could be considerably above the median VIX level. That is, investor expectations about the future are, nearly by definition, more volatile than today.

Looking at the prices of futures with different settlement dates at specific points in time provides a perspective on the variation in the market's view of expected VIX levels for various time periods. **Figure 12.2** and **Figure 12.3** show schematically the pattern of VIX futures prices on, respectively, 6 February 2013 and 22 August 2011.

In February 2013, the VIX was at slightly under 14%, and June through October VIX futures were priced in the range of 17%–20%. Investors seeking to roll February futures out to March would have had to pay up to extend their exposure another month. As in the case of commodities, such a roll cost erodes the buying power and, therefore, the long-term value of any fund tracking a front-month strategy. In the widely used S&P 500 Short-Term VIX Futures Index, about 5% of the portfolio is rolled each day. The Mid-Term VIX Futures Index has four futures in it (the 4th through 7th expiration) and only rolls 1.67% of its holding every day from the 4th to the 7th VIX futures. That roll cost eats into any returns of a holder of those indexes for longer than a few days.

VIX futures are not always in contango. In volatile market conditions, when the VIX is above median levels, and especially when it is higher than 25%, the VIX futures curve can move into backwardation, as it did in the third quarter of 2011. The profile of VIX futures prices in late August 2011, as shown in Figure 12.3, reflects a different picture from the pattern in February 2013. In such highly volatile periods, investors expect the market's volatility to revert to more normal levels in the future.

Figure 12.2.   Contango: VIX Futures Prices by Expiration Month, 6 February 2013

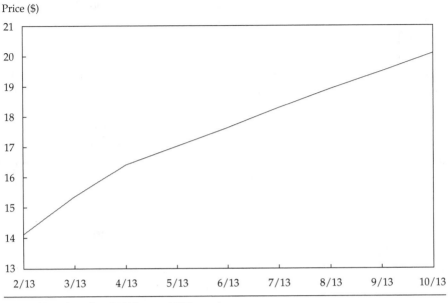

Price ($)

Source: Bloomberg (as of 6 February 2013).

Figure 12.3.   Backwardation: VIX Futures Prices by Expiration Month, 22 August 2011

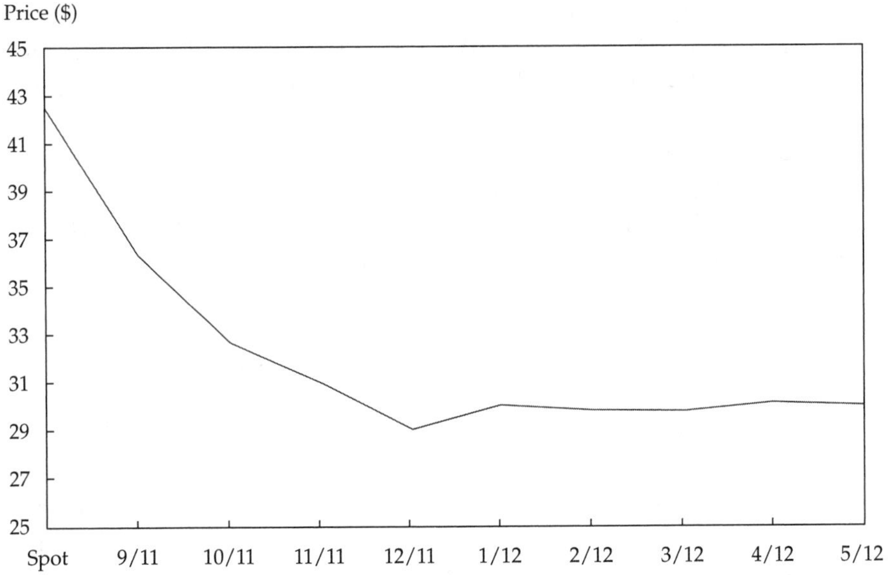

Price ($)

Source: Bloomberg (as of 22 August 2011).

The VIX term structure on 22 August 2011 showed the spot VIX at 42%, when concerns about a Greek default and its possible spillover into other eurozone debt markets and financial institutions shifted implied volatility significantly higher. September futures, however, are much lower, at 36%, and longer-term futures are close to 30%. This term structure is backwardation, when prices for futures with near-term expirations are higher than those with expirations further out. As Figure 12.3 shows, the biggest drop in the VIX was expected by the market in the first few months. Investors rolling long positions in VIX futures would have benefited by selling the contract nearest to expiration at a higher price than the one they would be buying with a longer-term expiration date. In this market environment, the process of rolling futures daily has a positive impact on return (i.e., instead of a cost to roll the futures contracts, there is a benefit—positive roll yield).

Differences between volatility trading tools exist not only because they reference expected VIX levels at different points into the future. On the one hand, short-term VIX futures strategies have a much larger component of their returns driven by the roll yield (positive or negative), which can be sizable if positions are held over extended periods. Thus, they are suited to short-horizon strategies (days or weeks in duration). On the other hand, strategies based on VIX futures that expire more than three months in the future have rolling cost properties that make them appealing for longer-horizon volatility exposure in an asset allocation context.

A comparison of the short-term futures and mid-term futures VIX roll costs is provided in **Figure 12.4**. The cost is the estimated cumulative roll yield cost, as reflected in VIX Futures Index returns, as of the VIX futures expiration each month back to the index inception. Figure 12.4 clearly shows that the roll yield cost component of the monthly returns for the short-term index, and exchange-traded products based on it, is much larger than that for the mid-term. The sign and magnitude of the roll yield cost is a reflection of market conditions. The largest yield costs came in years like 2012, when markets were quiet and VIX was low, but investors were worried about volatility rising in the future from US fiscal policy and uncertain economic conditions in Europe. In contrast, in the fall of 2011, when the VIX was high, the roll yield cost was positive because volatility was expected to return to normal (lower) levels in the months ahead.

The various features of the S&P 500 VIX Short-Term and Mid-Term Futures Indexes can be seen clearly in their historical correlations and betas relative to the S&P 500, shown in **Table 12.4**, and relative to the VIX, shown in **Table 12.5**. Both indexes have similar levels of correlation with the S&P 500 as the VIX.

Figure 12.4. Short-Term vs. Mid-Term VIX Futures' Estimated Monthly Roll Yield Cost, 17 February 2009–15 May 2014

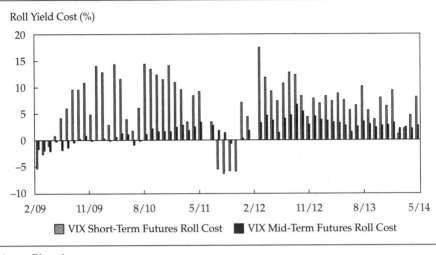

Source: Bloomberg.

Table 12.4. Correlation and Beta of VIX and S&P VIX Futures Indexes Relative to S&P 500, 22 January 2009–31 March 2014

Name	Correlation	Beta
VIX	−0.76	−4.58
S&P 500 VIX Short-Term Futures Index	−0.79	−2.73
S&P 500 VIX Mid-Term Futures ETN	−0.77	−1.27

Sources: Bloomberg and CBOE.

Table 12.5. Correlation and Beta of VIX and S&P VIX Futures Indexes Relative to VIX, 22 January 2009–31 March 2014

Name	Correlation	Beta
S&P 500 VIX Short-Term Futures Index	0.90	0.52
S&P 500 VIX Mid-Term Futures ETN	0.81	0.22

Sources: Bloomberg and CBOE.

The betas in relation to the S&P 500 are less negative than the VIX—namely, –2.68 for the S&P 500 VIX Short-Term Futures Index and –1.26 for the Mid-Term Index (the VIX itself moves more than four times as much as the S&P 500 on a typical day). These betas relative to the S&P 500 can be helpful in determining the notional exposure to an exchange-traded product for hedging equity exposure. Keep in mind that VIX futures ETFs have other components of returns (rolling costs) and do not have a strictly linear relationship with S&P 500 returns, so the beta provides an estimate based on the average relative moves in the historical period used in estimation. Also note that although both the VIX Short-Term Futures Index and Mid-Term Futures Index are highly positively correlated with the VIX, their betas are different. The beta relative to the VIX for the S&P 500 VIX Short-Term Futures Index is 0.53, which means that for a 1% move in the VIX, the short-term index would be expected to move 0.53%. The beta for the S&P 500 VIX Mid-Term Futures Index relative to the VIX is 0.23, about half that of the short-term index.

The best way to understand the performance of VIX futures indexes is to look at the return pattern of rolled VIX futures applying the index rules back through the financial crisis of 2007–2008 and also in the recent periods of lower volatility. **Figure 12.5** shows the quarterly returns updated weekly during the period April 2007–March 2014 for both the short-term and mid-term indexes against a chart of the S&P 500.[29] Notice how the returns are negative in most quarters, which reflects the cost of hedging with long volatility exposure. The returns can be as low as almost –50% per quarter for the short-term index and –25% for the mid-term index. Yet, when the markets shift into a higher-volatility regime, usually at the same time the S&P 500 falls sharply, performance of the VIX futures indexes swings to significantly positive, with returns of 100% or more for the short-term index and 50% or more for the mid-term index. This asymmetrical return pattern is the reason investors consider these tools for downside or tail risk management in equities. In contrast, inverse or short positions in these indexes can be a source of consistent returns as long as volatility is at normal or low levels, which is the majority of the time.

---

[29]Index returns are for illustrative purposes only and do not represent fund performance. Index returns do not reflect any management fees, transaction costs, or expenses.

Figure 12.5. Three-Month Rolling Returns for S&P 500 VIX Futures Indexes, 30 March 2007–31 March 2014

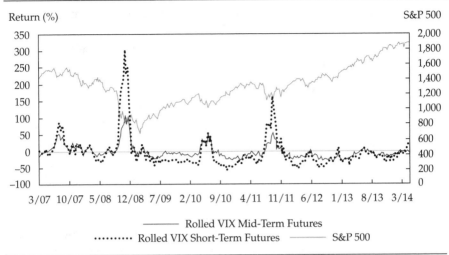

Note: For the period March 2007–February 2009, the returns are based on rolled VIX futures prices and accrued interest in three-month T-bills calculated by the methodology specified in the S&P VIX Short-Term and Mid-Term Futures calculations.
Sources: Bloomberg and CBOE.

Investment Applications of Tradable Volatility Products. Given the different features of VIX volatility indexes and VIX futures, the important task in an investment strategy is to align the investment objective and horizon with the appropriate type of volatility exposure. Some of the goals of using tradable volatility products based on the VIX futures indexes are the following:

- Act on changing market views of expected volatility: Use long or short positions in ETFs to speculate on a future level of VIX or implement tactical strategies across VIX futures ETFs.

- Help to manage downside equity risk: VIX futures have been negatively correlated with the S&P 500 and have tended to rise significantly during periods of market stress. ETFs benchmarked to VIX futures indexes can be used to reduce the equity risk in the portfolio with greater capital efficiency (and less risk) than adding cash or fixed-income exposure. That is, an allocation in the 5%–10% range has been shown to reduce risk similarly to taking positions of double that size in cash or fixed income.[30]

---

[30]Joanne M. Hill, "The Different Faces of Volatility Exposure in Portfolio Management," *Journal of Alternative Investments*, vol. 15, no. 3 (Winter 2013): 9–31.

- Seek to harvest returns from VIX futures rolling costs: VIX futures prices have been predominantly in contango when volatility is at a low or normal level. Returns of short-term volatility exposure through inverse ETFs on VIX futures indexes or from shorting long exposure ETFs can benefit, however, from rolling long VIX futures positions, as well as from declines in expected volatility.

In all cases, investors need to recognize that VIX futures ETFs are more volatile than equities on a standalone basis, include a significant return component of the rolling yield cost, and should not be used as buy-and-hold investments because of required frequent monitoring and rebalancing.

ETFs that package alternative strategies are a large component of new product launches as this book goes to press. Over the last several decades, indexing has grown in acceptance as a viable alternative to active management and ETFs have become a primary way of sourcing index-based strategies in traditional asset classes. We expect a similar process to occur in the area of alternatives. Hedge fund strategies and tactical tools in alternative asset classes are ever evolving, and we expect many will lend themselves to factor-based approaches that can be offered within the ETF structure for competitive fees. Many hedge fund strategies, however, involve derivative products and high degrees of leverage and depend intrinsically on portfolio manager discretion and nondisclosure. These strategies will be more difficult to provide outside the flexible hedge fund structure with its higher fees.

The Final Word on Alternatives ETFs: Look Closely Before You Leap. For those absolute return strategies and tactical tools that are packaged in ETFs, the investor must carry out the kind of due diligence on the drivers of the performance and risks that he or she would apply to a hedge fund strategy. ETFs do offer transparency of holdings, but many alternatives ETFs offer complex strategies that are suited primarily for sophisticated individuals and institutional investors.

13. Leveraged and Inverse ETFs

For many investors, some of the most interesting (and controversial) investment strategies made possible with ETFs have been those using leverage and those delivering the inverse returns from various asset classes (effectively, the performance of short exposure to indexes).

"Geared" ETFs, as they are often called, may seem novel, but leveraged and inverse strategies have been available in mutual fund form since the mid-1990s. They first appeared in ETFs in 2006, when ProShares was given the green light to launch ETFs with similar daily objective multipliers, such as +2, −1, and −2 times daily returns on indexes (shortened to 2X, −1X, −2X, and so forth). As of March 2014, as shown in **Table 13.1**, 266 geared ETFs with $42 billion in assets were operating in an enormous range of asset classes.

Most geared ETFs aim to provide their target multiple return (before fees and expenses) for a single day, so investors can depend on the funds having the target level of exposure regardless of the day they invest. These ETFs tend to track the multiple of the daily benchmark return tightly, but for longer periods, the leveraged or ETF returns may deviate from the target multiple times the benchmark return because of compounding.

This "compounding" effect on performance over time should be understood if investors are to effectively use these tools in an investment strategy. The magnitude and direction of the compounding effect on a buy-and-hold position in a geared fund depend on the length of time the position is held and the extent of trend and reversals in the returns of the benchmark over

Table 13.1.   Geared ETFs by Asset Class, as of 31 March 2014

Asset Class	No.
US equity	114
International equity	51
US fixed income	31
International fixed income	6
Commodities	33
Currency	13
Alternatives	16
Asset allocation	2

Source: ETF.com.

the holding period. On the one hand, when the benchmark trends upward or downward during the holding period, geared fund returns tend to be *greater than* the multiple of benchmark returns (e.g., more than 2 times the benchmark returns for a 2X fund). On the other hand, if the benchmark experiences high volatility during the period, with many reversals, the geared fund returns tend to be *less than* the multiple times the benchmark. **Table 13.2** illustrates the compounding effect.

In Table 13.2, the Index Daily Return column shows that an investment strategy that returned 10% a day for two consecutive days would generate a 21% gain over the two-day period; that is, compounding in the index has yielded a 1% improvement over a naive assumption that 10% for two days would be 20%. Similarly, in a downward-trending market, compounding can result in longer-term returns that are less negative than the sum of the individual daily returns. An investment that declined 10% a day for two consecutive days would have a –19% return, not –20%. In a volatile market scenario, compounding can result in long-term returns that are less than the sum of the individual daily returns. An investment that rose 10% on one day and declined 10% the next would have a –1% return, which is less than the 0% sum of the individual day returns.

Table 13.2. Compounding Effect on Geared Fund Performance

Day	Index Daily Return	2X Fund Daily Return
Upward trend		
1	10%	20%
2	10%	20%
Compound two-day return	+21%	+44%
Downward trend		
1	–10%	–20%
2	–10%	–20%
Compound two-day return	–19%	–36%
Volatile market		
1	10%	20%
2	–10%	–20%
Compound two-day return	–1%	–4%

Compounding in leveraged funds can result in gains or losses that occur much faster and to a greater degree, as shown in the 2X Fund Daily Return column. In an upward-trending market, compounding can result in long-term leveraged returns that are greater than 2 times the return of the unleveraged investment. A leveraged fund that grew 20% a day (2 × 10% index gain) for two consecutive days would have a 44% gain, not 2 times the 21% compound gain of the Index Daily Return. In a downward trending market, compounding results in 2X leveraged fund returns that are less negative than 2 times the return of the unleveraged investment. A 2X leveraged fund that declined 20% a day (2 × 10% index decline) for two consecutive days would have a −36% return. This return is less negative than 2 times the 19% compound loss of the unleveraged investment. In a volatile market, compounding can result in leveraged longer-term returns that are less than 2 times the return of the unleveraged investment. A 2X leveraged fund that rose 20% one day (2 × 10% index gain) and declined 20% the next (2 × 10% index decline) would generate a −4% return. This return is a greater loss than 2 times the −1% compound return of the unleveraged investment.

This example is useful for illustrating the role compounding plays in returns, but it is unrealistic because the moves shown of 10% in a series of days are uncommon for benchmarks on which leveraged and inverse funds are based. One of the most common uses of inverse funds is to hedge interest rate or equity risk. To show how ETFs perform over time relative to their daily target multipliers, we first provide some examples for a three-month period for the inverse and inverse leveraged ETFs most widely used to hedge interest rate risk. The ProShares UltraShort 20+ Year Treasury ETF (TBT) and ProShares Short 20+ Year Treasury ETF (TBF) have the objective of −2X and −1X the daily returns of the Barclays Capital U.S. 20+ Year Treasury Bond Index (BarCap Index). They expect, therefore, to show profits on days when this index falls in value as long-term Treasury yields are rising.

Figure 13.1 shows the cumulative performance of the benchmark and capital returns for TBF and TBT between the end of June and the end of September 2013. In the first six weeks of the period (through 19 August), the BarCap Index posted a −6.67% return and TBF returned 6.58% whereas TBT gained 13.44%. These returns were close to −1X and −2X times the benchmark return; the index was in a consistent downtrend over the period. By the end of the quarter, however, the benchmark had reversed some of its losses and only showed a −2.70% return. TBF and TBT, with returns of 1.84% and 3.47%, respectively, were affected by negative compounding effects and delivered less than −1X and −2X the index return over the period. If the investors had rebalanced their positions during the quarter, the compounding

Figure 13.1. BarCap Index vs. TBT and TBF: Cumulative Returns for Q3 2013

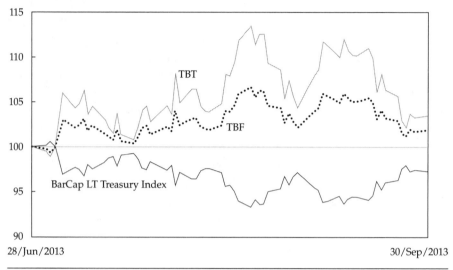

effects might have been less. An important fact to remember is that holding an inverse fund as a hedge when the benchmark index posts positive returns can result in losses related to the move in the index as well as any compounding effects related to volatility over the period.

As an example of inverse and leveraged inverse funds for hedging equity risk, **Figure 13.2** shows the cumulative capital returns for the third quarter of 2013 for the S&P 500 and the ProShares Short S&P500 ETF (SH) and the ProShares UltraShort S&P500 ETF (SDS), which are, respectively, −1X and −2X daily objective S&P 500 inverse funds. The figure shows the extent to which the inverse ETFs move opposite to the returns in the S&P 500. Over the period, the S&P 500 posted a 5.24% return whereas SH posted a loss, −5.34%, as did SDS, −10.67%. Because this period was not highly volatile for the S&P 500, the returns were close to the daily objective multiplier times the index.

Figure 13.2.   S&P 500 vs. SDS and SH: Cumulative Returns for Q3 2013, 28 June 2013–30 September 2013

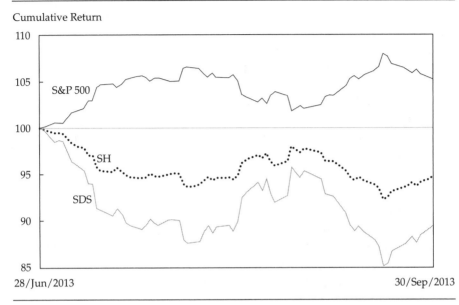

Holding and Rebalancing Leveraged and Inverse ETFs for Long Periods

Investors may choose to use leveraged and inverse funds for long holding periods, despite the compounding effects, as long as certain conditions are true. For example, an investor may understand the impact of compounding on performance over time but have a view that the underlying index will be moving in a trend upward or downward and the investor is hoping to benefit from the positive impact of compounding in a trending market. Alternatively, an investor may understand that the ETF may deliver a return that is not exactly the daily objective multiple if the position is held over a long period but is willing to accept the risk of some variation around the daily target in exchange for the potential benefit of the ETF exposure.

Some investors who hold leveraged and inverse funds for long horizons may be using a strategy to monitor and rebalance the position so that they come close to the daily objective multiplier over long horizons. Rebalancing is necessary and can be effective in bringing the position returns in line with the target multiplier over longer periods.[31] Such a strategy involves periodi-

---

[31]"Rebalancing Leveraged and Inverse Funds," *Eighth Annual Guide to Exchange-Traded Funds*, Institutional Investor Journals (Fall 2009): 67–76.

cally adding to, or reducing, the size of the geared ETF positions to realign exposure to the underlying index. This rebalancing does involve transaction costs and has tax consequences that need to be considered. Usually investors base the decision to rebalance on the gap between the index return and fund return. An investor may have a trigger for this gap—say, 5%—and when the gap reaches the trigger, the investor rebalances in an amount equal to the difference between the initial position (or last rebalanced position value) times (1+ the index return) and the current position. Therefore, if the index has moved to a higher value than the position, the investor will add to it (cover the losses), and if the index has fallen relative to the leveraged/inverse ETF position, the investor will reduce the position (taking the gains).

Holdings and Expenses

Geared ETFs that offer leveraged exposure typically invest most of their capital in securities of the benchmark index or T-bills held at a third-party custodian together with a position in either long futures or total return swaps consistent with the ETF benchmark.

Swaps are negotiated agreements with bank counterparties. Although some counterparty risk is implied in these arrangements, most managers of geared ETFs have terms in their agreements to settle up any gains and losses daily with their counterparties. So, credit exposure is effectively limited to a one-day move in the benchmark index.

For a futures-based geared ETF, the fund must be rebalanced at the end of the day so that it has the correct benchmark exposure for the next trading day. For example, suppose a 2X daily objective S&P 500 fund starts the day with $100 million and holds $200 million in notional exposure. Assuming the index moves up 3%, the futures positions may appreciate $6 million to an exposure value of $206 million. With the $6 million gain, the fund now has assets of $106 million (2 × 3%) and needs to hold future positions of $212 million to provide 2X of the next day's return. Therefore, the ETF manager will do a rebalance trade close to the end of the trading day to buy $6 million more of futures exposure so the fund can participate in 2X of the benchmark returns on the following day. Both leveraged and inverse ETFs also must be rebalanced, with the ETFs buying exposure when benchmark returns move higher and selling exposure for days of benchmark declines. Usually a +2X leveraged ETF has rebalancing requirements similar in size to those of a –1X inverse ETF. (Stated differently, a –2X daily objective ETF requires larger rebalancing trades to stay in line with its daily objective multiplier target than a +2X ETF.)

Note that, as specialized vehicles, most geared exchange-traded products are significantly more expensive than plain-vanilla ETFs that track simple indexes. The average leveraged fund expense ratio as of 31 March 2014 was 1.03%, and the average inverse fund expense ratio was 0.99%. This cost is in addition to any embedded costs that may be incurred by the fund for swap arrangements.

Strategy Applications of Geared ETFs

Leveraged and inverse index exposure in a liquid and transparent ETF can be used in a variety of ways and for both short- and long-term horizons. Given the high levels of trading activity for these ETFs, the primary use is probably as short-term tactical trading tools. Investors may also, however, regularly use leveraged and inverse ETFs as key components of a long-term portfolio strategy—for example, to pursue returns and manage the risks of long equity and fixed-income positions. Given the daily objective of the target multiplier, the ongoing strategy applications over a long-horizon require monitoring and rebalancing to achieve that target multiplier.

Following is a summary of the most common applications of leveraged and inverse ETFs:

- Pursue returns based on a short-term tactical view (long or short) of an index

- Overweight or underweight an index exposure—such as a particular market-cap segment, sector, or country—by using leverage and thereby avoid the need to change other positions in the portfolio

- Hedge or reduce risk, either as a short-term tactical hedge or for long-term risk management with monitoring and rebalancing

- Execute an index spread strategy to capture the relative returns of two indexes. For example, an investor might wish to express a view that financial stocks are likely to outperform energy stocks or that emerging market equities will outperform US large-cap equities.

- Isolate the alpha from active strategies. The active risk component of an equity strategy (alpha) can be isolated by using an inverse or leveraged inverse index ETF to hedge the index or beta risk of the benchmark for that strategy.

14.   The Future of ETFs

Few investment products have achieved the kind of market penetration and growth that exchange-traded funds have attained in just over two decades. The achievement is even more impressive in light of the turbulence of the period—from the technology bubble of the 1990s to the 2007–09 global financial crisis. At the current pace of growth, ETF assets in the United States will likely top $3 trillion within a few years of this writing and will quickly represent almost 15% of mutual fund assets. The dollar volume of ETF trading activity is regularly more than 25% of exchange trading activity in the United States and is gaining similar ground globally.

In some ways, the growth of the ETF market is a manifestation of the battle for the heart and soul of investing. ETFs have boosted index-based investing tremendously. Their widespread adoption has the potential to shake up legacy practices that have been entrenched in asset management for many years—including the role of consultants in finding investment products, mutual fund distribution through financial advisers and registered investment advisers, and the central role of actively managed, bottom-up, stock and bond management.

Consider what smartphones have done for personal communication, computing, location services, and photography by integrating several formerly separate functions into one device. In a less dramatic but similar fashion, ETFs have democratized and altered investing by integrating attractive features of portfolio management—ease of access to broad and narrow financial market segments, cost effectiveness, transparency of prices, and return measurement, liquidity, and tax efficiency. In the same way that the early smartphones were first the province of tech-savvy young adults, the early days of ETFs saw adoption by sophisticated investors, including trading-oriented institutional investors and hedge funds. Today, we see those early adopters joined by all the important classes of investors: institutions, advisers (both RIAs and financial advisers at broker/dealers), and self-directed retail investors. Whereas in the early days, ETF managers came from the ranks of institutional index managers—such as State Street and the old Barclays Global Investors (now BlackRock)—today, we see the largest mutual fund managers entering the space, including PIMCO, JPMorgan, Fidelity, Goldman Sachs, and T. Rowe Price.

Nevertheless, obstacles still impede ETF asset growth, and if the obstacles were removed, the adoption of ETFs would accelerate. In the United States, a major obstacle is inability of most 401(k)/defined-contribution investment programs to handle ETFs and the lack of expertise in ETF analysis among the institutional consulting community. In addition, the current regulatory framework allows for ETF issuance and trading as a subcategory of *both* mutual fund and equity products, creating a Byzantine approval and oversight environment.

Furthermore, although exchange access is viewed by most investors as a plus, it does disrupt the existing distribution process for mutual funds, which has been, by and large, successful. Because ETFs are purchased from broker/dealer intermediaries, ETF issuers have no easy way of knowing who specifically is buying their products, which makes it difficult to reward distributors for success in sales and education efforts (not to mention getting good information and regulatory documents into investor hands). The low fees of ETFs leave less scope for paying for marketing and distribution services, which have been so important to the asset-gathering process of mutual funds and institutional active management. Low fees are great for investors, but they make large marketing campaigns difficult to mount.

To explore the future of ETFs, the best starting point is to review the sources of their growth in the first 20+ years. The first ETFs were built for a specific reason—to provide institutions with liquid access to equity indexes, such as the S&P 500 Index and NASDAQ 100 Index. These early ETFs appealed to a narrow range of institutional investors and hedge funds that preferred a stock-like trading vehicle over using index futures or separately managed accounts for long holding periods. In the 1990s, the indexes broadened to include international markets, which were much more challenging to access through futures than were US markets, with the result that these sophisticated investors gained much better access to global markets than investors who were not using ETFs.

As we entered the 2000s, ETF sponsors developed products in fixed income and other asset classes and professionalized their distribution strategies. The adviser community started using ETFs for asset allocation, and by the end of that volatile decade, surveys of institutions and financial advisers showed that the use of ETFs was increasing for everything from intraday speculation to long-term buy-and-hold exposure. The value of these ETFs became quickly apparent for adjusting asset class exposures; advisers and institutional investors shifted from the old buy-and-hold asset class "bucket" mentality into one that was adaptive to changing market conditions. This last phase of growth was also the time when individual investors began using ETFs directly and through their financial advisers at brokerage firms. In some cases, their understanding of how the ETFs could and should be used was limited, especially with some of the more complex ETFs, such as those that use derivatives to achieve leveraged and inverse payoffs and commodity ETFs. In these instances, the Financial Industry Regulatory Authority and the US SEC stepped in to suggest sales guidelines and to emphasize the importance of learning about the features of the ETFs before investing. With this regulatory scrutiny, it became apparent that ETFs had arrived.

Drivers of Broader ETF Adoption

Today, institutions, RIAs, FAs, and self-directed individual investors are all using ETFs in increasingly interesting ways. Institutions have always been big users of ETFs, but historically, they had a short-term focus, with primary uses being "cash equitization" and "transition management." For the next decade, growing use by institutions for core exposure will be an important component of the ETF growth story. This trend is likely to include the largest pension funds, those that were early adopters for international equity and commodity access. But it will also include insurance companies and small pensions, endowments, and foundations, which previously relied heavily on consultants to select their investment managers. Along the way, we expect most hedge funds to continue using ETFs for managing risk and macro-exposures, primarily on the short side or in global macro strategies.

Recent surveys by Greenwich Associates of institutional investor use of ETFs show an increase in use, and further increases are expected in the future. The 2014 survey indicated that

> nearly half of institutional ETF users now allocate more than 10% of total assets to ETFs with ETFs gaining traction in asset classes outside equities, especially in fixed income, where changes in market structure could boost ETF use.[32]

ETF holding periods are also lengthening. The 2011 survey indicated that only 20% of institutional ETF users held positions for more than two years. In the 2014 survey, the share of institutions reporting average holding periods of two years or longer had jumped to 49%.

High-net-worth and individual retirement assets advised by the FA and RIA communities are also expected to continue to drive growth in ETF investments. The share of assets that are managed on behalf of individual investors for wealth management and retirement purposes has been growing,

---

[32]Greenwich Associates, "ETFs: An Evolving Toolset for U.S. Institutions," Greenwich Report (12 May 2014).

especially when compared with defined-benefit pension assets. Investment advisers are sources of ETF asset growth in four areas:

1. More FAs and RIAs are including ETFs in their investment strategies for both tactical and strategic investment objectives.

2. As ETFs expand into more categories of indexes, including some that have significant elements of active management, the share ETFs represent of the investment portfolios of FA and RIA clients is increasing.

3. Traditional mutual fund managers are launching actively managed ETFs for their primary fund products in cases where these funds can be adapted to the ETF fund structure and holdings disclosure.

4. Managed portfolios of ETFs are becoming a major part of the asset management industry. "ETF managers" may be specialty managers who offer strategies for a fee on broker/dealer platforms. They often distribute to RIAs and even, in some cases, institutions. Also, traditional asset management companies are developing asset allocation/multi-asset strategies that use ETFs for implementation. These strategies can be offered to insurance companies or through the same broker/dealer platforms used by the ETF specialty managers.

The final ETF growth engine is direct investing in ETFs by individuals who invest or manage their retirement assets through brokerage accounts. More direct ETF investment is likely because of the diversity of ETF products and the increased availability of education about their features and investment uses. ETF sponsor websites, broker/dealer research arms, and ETF research services (such as ETF.com, ETF Trends, and Morningstar) provide educational guides and resources for screening and evaluating ETFs. As individual investors observe greater ETF use within their professionally managed investment portfolios and as the mutual fund industry offers more of their successful strategies packaged in ETFs, we will see stories similar to what happened at Vanguard and PIMCO. These firms are seeing an increasing share of their investors from a wide range of channels elect to use their ETF products.

Falling Distribution Barriers

Changes in the way ETFs are sold could also have a significant impact on growth. Best estimates suggest that, although institutions account for 50%–55% of ETF assets, only about 18% of institutions own any ETFs at all. That situation is changing as bespoke institutional products designed to serve the needs of specific institutions are launched. In short, ETFs have become a viable wrapper alternative for separately managed institutional accounts. Pension consultants do not have the same in-depth coverage of ETFs, however, that they have for evaluating separately managed accounts offered by asset managers or for hedge funds. This situation is changing, but slowly.

Also, until 2013, insurance companies could not own bond ETFs because of an accounting rule that counted all ETFs as "equities," which forced insurance companies to take a capital charge on their books for ETF assets. Now, bond ETFs count as bonds, and insurance companies are moving quickly to use bond ETFs in risk management. Similarly, defined-contribution—401(k)—accounts have historically been restricted to mutual fund options because of obstacles to exchange-traded products in portfolio accounting practices. ETF sponsors and 401(k) providers are working hard, however, to develop back-end solutions so ETFs can be viable in the plans.

Some of the barriers in the advisory market are also fading away. Mutual funds typically paid a fee to broker/dealers whenever these firms' advisers put clients into funds. Low-cost ETFs had no such payment arrangements. Recently, tremendous growth has occurred in the use by financial advisers of fee-based ETF managers who build portfolios of ETFs that other advisers can follow. The managers implement their strategies primarily with ETFs and pay distribution fees, similar to the payment arrangements long associated with mutual funds, to broker/dealers for asset flows. This segment has gone from zero to $100 billion in a few years.

"Smart Beta," Alternative, and Multi-Asset ETF Strategies

Another way in which ETFs are capturing assets from mutual funds and separately managed accounts is simply through product innovation. Issuers are pushing forward aggressively into new ETF products that use rules-based strategies built around one or multiple investment themes to compete head-to-head with traditional active managers. The success of these quant strategies will always be market dependent, but recent asset flows suggest that the strategies have been successful in capturing investor interest.

A few years ago, we did not even use the term "smart beta" for these types of equity strategies; we called them "quantitative investing" or "enhanced indexing." The basic idea has remained the same since the 1990s: to identify one or more factors or investment themes, then build a quantitative model for the security selection and weighting process, and wedge the approach into an index by reweighting the stocks in the index according to the quantitative model. For example, in equities, the factors might be company fundamentals, high dividend yields, high dividend growth, stocks with buyback programs, hedge fund stock holdings, low volatility, high beta; the choices are unlimited. These factors are similar to those used by good discretionary managers at mutual fund firms, but ETFs using systematic approaches to selection and to rebalancing security holdings have become the new hot area for ETF launches and asset growth. Because this stock-investing activity closely resembles what mutual fund managers do for higher fees, it is the area where they are most likely to be threatened.

The smart beta concept has been extended to asset classes other than equities but with limited success to date. Consider bonds: The structure of the fixed-income market is inherently less efficient than the structure of the equity market. Thus, both the data and implementation components of rules-based strategies are more of a challenge when applied to bonds. At the same time, traditional active fixed-income mutual fund managers, having seen the growth of PIMCO's fixed-income ETFs, are following close behind. In some cases, they are trying to speed up their ETF launches by partnering with ETF sponsors to offer actively managed ETFs with disclosed holdings. For example, State Street Global Advisors (SSgA) has partnered with Blackstone in an ETF that focuses on the leveraged loan market (SPDR Blackstone/ GSO Senior Loan ETF, SRLN). SSgA has also partnered with DoubleLine, a large mutual fund fixed-income manager to launch an ETF (Doubleline Total Return Tactical ETF, TOTL).[33]

Integrating active and quantitative investment approaches is going to be a key component of the further evolution and growth of commodity, asset allocation, and alternative strategy ETFs. Although several commodity indexes have taken small steps toward "smarter" indexing by algorithmically managing the impact of contango and backwardation, progress overall has been slow. There is much less of a pipeline for smart beta products outside of equities and fixed income. Investment managers specializing in asset allocation and liquid alternatives are working with mutual funds as well as ETF managers to innovate to meet the growing interest in adding more of these strategies, widely considered to be diversifying to equity risk, into the portfolio mix.

The increasingly diverse range of quasi-active investment strategies packaged in ETFs, however, raises some big red flags. If history is any indication, half or more of these strategy index/active ETFs are destined to underperform market-capitalization-weighted indexes and regularly rebalanced target asset mix strategies even before fees; after fees are deducted, the chances of success may be even lower. Although these strategy index ETFs have the preferred ETF features of access, transparency, and tax efficiency, they still rely on the success of the investment process. Therefore, as with the selection of

---

[33]Cinthia Murphy, "Gundlach, SSgA Team for New Bond ETF," ETF.com (2 June 2014).

active mutual fund or institutional strategies, due diligence as to the investment process and the risks of the fund should be the starting point in considering their fit in an investment program.

The Final Word

In conclusion, we believe that ETF growth in the coming decade will most likely come primarily from the largest asset ETFs being used by an increasingly broad clientele for an increasingly larger portion of their portfolios. New ETF launches—be they traditional active management or smart beta—may help speed the pace but are not likely to be the market drivers. History suggests that long-term financial market conditions favor low-cost, index-based ETFs that provide market performance in a liquid package. In low-volatility markets, low-cost indexing has historically flourished. Conversely, ETFs' trading features make them more valuable in volatile market conditions, when investors are looking for positions that can easily be altered when market conditions change. In either case, diversification wins, and ETFs provide it.

Does all we have discussed about the advantages of ETFs sound like a death knell for active investing? We think not. Since the invention of the index fund, the popular financial press and industry pundits alike have been announcing the death of the bottom-up stock picker. Yet, hope for active management springs eternal. Rational or not, people will always have an enormous appetite for the promise of active investing, even if the statistics suggest that, *as a class*, active investors underperform. The reason is that in every survey of 1,000 active managers, some, of course, deliver enormous risk-adjusted outperformance. And some investors—institutional and retail alike—will always seek out those managers who can pick the next hot stock or the next undervalued municipal bond. The rise of ETFs simply makes it harder for those active managers who do not deliver to remain competitive.

In fact, the continued appeal of active management is likely to mean that a large chunk of ETF asset growth will be driven by the expansion of ETFs into active strategies that push into more traditional mutual fund space, such as smart beta, alternatives, and asset allocation. Also, keep in mind that active management is part of the gambit of ETF managers who are paid a fee to tactically allocate ETFs based on their allocation and valuation models.

Nevertheless, the success of the top-down, factor-based, or thematic active strategies in ETFs depends on market dynamics and the quality of the investment approach. Nothing about bolting "ETF" on the front of an active management strategy will make it better.

Finally, the importance of efficiency in investing is critical in considering the future of ETFs. It is nearly axiomatic in economic terms that the more efficient products, market structures, companies, and processes win over their less efficient competitors. Regardless of the market environment, management fees, trading costs, transfer agency fees, and other charges destroy investor capital. The efficiency of ETFs not only helps end investors, it also helps financial advisers who charge fees for their wealth management services.

Moreover, increased competition will only accelerate the efficiency of ETFs. Competition among ETF managers has always been intense and has kept up the pace of innovation in investment products at a reasonable cost. Now that more asset managers are becoming part of the ETF manager club, competition can only continue to benefit investors. Being an intelligent user of ETFs requires some education, but it is rare to find an investor who tries ETFs and then turns away from the product disappointed. Rather, most new users quickly begin to look for more areas of their portfolio in which they can use an ETF to fit their investment needs.

Appendix A. The Global Footprint of ETFs and ETPs

Deborah Fuhr
Managing Partner, ETFGI
Assistance provided by Shane Kelly, CFA, and Matthew Murray

The exchange-traded fund/exchange-traded product industry is global, with products offered in each country used by investors worldwide. The global nature of ETFs and ETPs is relevant to providers, investors, and other participants in the ecosystem that supports the industry. Many providers of ETFs/ETPs headquartered in the United States have a multiregional or global product and sales footprint and often register and cross-list their US-domiciled ETFs/ETPs in other countries and regions. Investors around the world often own ETFs/ETPs domiciled in their home country as well as those issued in the United States and other jurisdictions.[34]

ETFs are defined here as products structured as regulated funds; other ETPs are structured as notes, partnerships, grantor trusts, and commodity pools. Being specific and transparent about the structure of each product is important because for most investors, regulated funds have tax and regulatory treatments that are different from those of other structures. In some cases, non-fund products require knowing the identity of the underlying investors, which, in the case of private banks, can be a problem.

The global ETF/ETP industry, as measured by assets under management, has been growing at a 27.1% annual rate for the past 10 years. As **Figure A.1** shows, at the end of September 2014, 5,463 ETFs and ETPs, with 10,510 listings and assets of $2.63 trillion from 225 providers were listed on 61 exchanges in 49 countries. Of the total assets, 94.4% was invested in the 3,868 ETFs and only 5.6%, or $148 billion, was invested in the 1,595 products that used a non-mutual-fund structure or were ETPs.

Assets in the ETF/ETP industry are coming close to surpassing the size of the hedge fund industry. The difference in assets narrowed from $230 billion at the end of 2013 to $193 billion at the end of September 2014. The global ETF/ETP industry, which has existed for almost 25 years, continues to grow at a faster rate than the global hedge fund industry, which has existed

---

[34]This appendix refers to data from the ETFGI September 2014 global ETF and ETP industry insights report, the ETFGI 2013 report on institutional users of ETFs and ETPs, and ETFGI's databases. All amounts are expressed in US dollars.

Figure A.1. Global ETF and ETP Asset Growth, 2000–2014

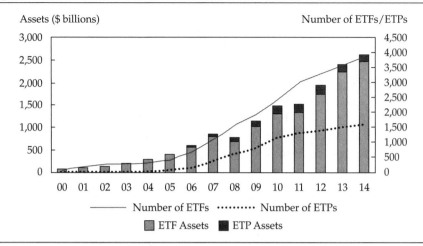

Sources: ETFGI data sourced from ETF/ETP sponsors, exchanges, regulatory filings, Thomson Reuters/Lipper, Bloomberg, publicly available sources, and data generated in-house.

for 65 years. Assets in the global ETF/ETP industry are only $193 billion smaller than the assets in the global hedge fund industry.

The global hedge fund industry reached a new record high of $2.819 trillion invested in 8,367 funds at the end of September 2014, according to a report published by Hedge Fund Research, Inc. (HFRI). Net inflows into hedge funds through the end of September 2014 were $72.7 billion. Assets in the hedge fund industry increased by $190 billion, or 7%, in the first nine months of 2014. Hedge fund performance in 2014, through the end of September, as measured by the HFRI Fund Weighted Composite Index, was +3.07%, whereas the S&P 500 Index was +8.34% over the same period.

As of September 2014, the global ETF/ETP market had $2.625 trillion invested in 5,463 ETFs and ETPs. During 2014, through the end of September, ETFs and ETPs globally gathered a record $199 billion in net new assets, more than double the amount of net new assets gathered by hedge funds. Assets in ETFs/ETPs increased by $227 billion, or 9.5%, during the first nine months of 2014, a faster growth rate than hedge funds during the same period.

A 3% annual rate of increase has occurred in the number of institutional investors that reported using globally listed ETFs and ETPs in the past five years.[35] Institutional investors numbering 3,590 located in 52 countries and

---

[35]This conclusion is based on our analysis of global regulatory filings and mutual fund holdings during 2013. See Thomson Reuters Lipper share ownership database.

6,480 mutual funds in 46 countries reported using one or more ETFs or ETPs in 2013.

The United States is the home to two-thirds of the institutional investors that reported holding ETFs/ETPs in 2013. Indeed, the United States is the dominant country in terms of ETF and ETP assets under management, accounting for 70.9% of the $2.63 trillion invested globally in these products. Many institutional investors around the world are investing in US-listed ETFs/ETPs. Many of the ETF/ETP providers have built a multiregional or global business by registering for sale and cross-listing US-listed ETFs and ETNs in other countries as well as creating products domiciled locally in countries and regions around the world.

Some 2,522 institutional investors held 55% of US-listed ETF and ETP assets at the end of 2013. Large firms, those with more than $10 billion in overall AUM, represented only 11.2% of institutional ETF and ETP users by count, although in terms of dollar holdings, these large firms accounted for 66.2% of reported assets. In contrast, the smallest firms, those with less than $500 million in overall AUM, accounted for 52.7% of ETF and ETP users but only 7.9% of the assets invested in ETFs/ETPs.

Institutions in 49 countries reported holding at least one US-listed ETF or ETP as of the end of 2013. The majority of these institutions reported holding more than one ETF or ETP. In the United States, the use of ETFs and ETPs by registered investment advisers is significant, accounting for 38% of US-listed assets at the end of 2013 according to Broadridge Financial Solutions. Individual purchasers also use US-listed ETFs and ETPs. They accounted for an estimated 6% of overall assets at the end of 2013.

Equity ETFs and ETPs number 2,832 globally and account for 76.6%, or $2.01 trillion, of the global asset total of $2.62 trillion. The 812 fixed-income products account for $392 billion, or 14.9% of the assets, whereas the 744 commodity products have $127 billion, or 4.8% of all assets. The 175 actively managed ETFs and ETPs, with $26 billion in assets, are still a small part of the industry; they account for only 1% of overall assets.

The top five ETF and ETP providers, out of 225 ranked by assets, all have global ETF and/or ETP businesses and accounted for 75.4% of the $2.63 trillion invested in ETFs and ETPs at the end of September 2014. The remaining 220 providers each had less than a 2% market share. The firm iShares, with $980 billion, reflecting a 37.3% market share, is the largest ETF/ETP provider in terms of assets. SPDR (Standard & Poor's Depositary Receipt) ETFs, with $432 billion and a 16.4% market share, are second. Third is Vanguard, with $407 billion and a 15.5% market share, and fourth is

Powershares, with $93 billion. Deutsche Bank (DB) X-trackers ETFs, with $68 billion, are fifth in size of assets.

Only 7%, or 389, of ETFs/ETPs listed globally have been able to gather more than $1 billion in assets. This small minority accounts for a combined total of $2.10 trillion, or 80.1%, of global ETF/ETP assets. Fewer than a third of all ETFs and ETPs, or 1,735, have gathered more than $100 million in assets, the amount often cited as the breakeven level.

ETFs listed globally have an asset-weighted average expense ratio of 0.31%. The cheapest products, with a ratio of 0.24%, track fixed-income indexes; the most expensive are leveraged ETFs with a ratio of 0.87%. There are 80 ETFs with an expense ratio less than 0.1% and 136 ETFs with an expense ratio greater than 1%.

S&P Dow Jones has the largest amount of ETF/ETP assets tracking its benchmarks—$754 billion, reflecting a 28.7% market share. MSCI is second, $382 billion and a 14.5% market share, followed by Barclays, $230 billion and an 8.7% market share.

From January through September 2014, brokers globally reported 9,079,445 trades in US- and European-listed ETFs and ETPs with a dollar value totaling $9.67 trillion. Merrill Lynch, with $2.15 trillion in trades, reported the largest volume. It was followed by KCG Holdings, with $1.3 trillion. The top 20 brokers, as ranked by reported volumes, accounted for 94.4% of advertised trades, and 228 other brokers collectively accounted for the remaining 5.6%.

As of the end of 2013, the global ETF industry accounted for 7.5% of the global mutual fund industry, which had 76,200 mutual funds with $30.05 trillion in AUM.[36]

Table A.1 provides a breakdown of ETFs and ETPs as to number, number of listings, and AUM by region and country. The rest of this appendix provides brief overviews of the ETF and ETP industries in Canada, Latin America, Europe, the Asia Pacific (ex Japan) region, Japan, and the Middle East and Africa region. The universe outside the United States at the end of September 2014 consisted of 3,813 ETFs/ETPs listed on 58 exchanges, with more than $760 billion in AUM and listings in 48 countries.

---

[36]Investment Company Institute.

Table A.1.   ETFs/ETPs Listed by Region and Country

Region/Country	# of ETFs/ETPs	# of Total Listings	Assets ($ millions)
North America			
Canada	285	407	59,392
United States	1,536	1,536	1,700,965
Total	1,821	1,943	1,760,357
Latin America			
Brazil	15	15	1,185
Chile	2	108	27
Colombia	2	5	1,541
Mexico	19	470	8,250
Peru	—	2	—
Total	38	600	11,002
Europe			
Austria	1	20	112
Belgium	1	34	44
Finland	3	3	203
France	291	504	56,306
Germany	567	1,806	146,521
Greece	3	3	40
Hungary	1	1	11
Iceland	2	2	15
Ireland	1	3	37
Italy	62	837	4,605
Netherlands	22	162	1,331
Norway	5	13	470
Poland	1	3	21
Portugal	3	3	131
Romania	1	1	0
Russia	8	9	35
Spain	11	72	1,911
Sweden	26	108	4,020
Switzerland	296	1,105	45,560

(continued)

Table A.1. ETFs/ETPs Listed by Region and Country (continued)

Region/Country	# of ETFs/ETPs	# of Total Listings	Assets ($ millions)
Turkey	17	17	83
United Kingdom	671	1,479	156,111
Total	1,993	6,185	417,566
Asia Pacific			
Australia	68	89	5,972
China	79	79	25,001
Hong Kong	93	130	339,696
India	39	39	1,670
Indonesia	4	4	37
Japan	128	170	77,306
Malaysia	4	5	305
New Zealand	5	5	294
Philippines	1	1	17
Singapore	31	97	2,514
South Korea	146	146	18,447
Taiwan	19	22	4,684
Thailand	16	16	171
Total	633	803	170,113
Middle East and Africa			
Botswana	—	2	—
Ghana	—	1	—
Israel	534	534	32,655
Mauritius	—	1	—
Namibia	—	4	—
Nigeria	—	1	—
Saudi Arabia	3	3	16
South Africa	64	64	5,994
United Arab Emirates	1	1	16
Total	602	607	38,680

Sources: ETFGI data sourced from ETF/ETP sponsors, exchanges, regulatory filings, Thomson Reuters Lipper, Bloomberg, publicly available sources, and data generated in-house.

Canada

Canada listed the first ETF in 1990, three years before the SPDR S&P 500 (SPY) became the first ETF listed in the United States. The first ETF listed on the Toronto Stock Exchange (TSX) was the Toronto 35 Index Participation Fund, which tracks the TSX 35 Equity Index. In 2000, this ETF was merged with the Hundred Index Participation Fund, which tracks the TSX 100, to create the iUnits S&P/TSE Index Participation Fund, which has since been renamed the iShares CDN S&P/TSX 60 Index Fund (XIU CN).

As **Figure A.2** shows, the Canadian industry had 317 ETFs, with 439 listings and assets of $65 billion from nine providers listed on the TSE. Although the Canadian ETF/ETP industry launched the first ETF and, based on AUM, has been growing at a 26.8% annual rate for the past 10 years, it accounts for only 2.5% of global ETF/ETP assets.

In Canada, nearly two-thirds of the industry's assets are invested in products providing exposure to equity benchmarks, slightly more than a quarter are in fixed income, and 2% are in commodities. The 41 active ETFs account for 4.4% of overall assets. Canada has nontransparent active ETFs, something for which asset managers in the United States have been trying for more than six years to gain approval from the US SEC.

Only 4%, or 13 ETFs/ETPs, have more than $1 billion in assets, but they account for a combined total of $29 billion, or 44.9%, of the Canadian

Figure A.2.   Canadian ETF Asset Growth, 2000–2014

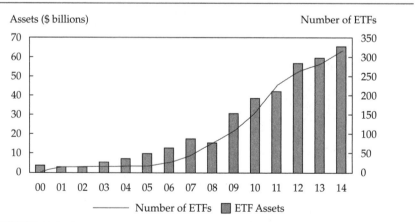

Sources: ETFGI data sourced from ETF/ETP sponsors, exchanges, regulatory filings, Thomson Reuters Lipper, Bloomberg, publicly available sources, and data generated in-house.

©2015 The CFA Institute Research Foundation

industry's total assets. Slightly more than one-third of the products have more than $100 million in assets, often considered the breakeven level for ETFs.

ETFs and ETPs in Canada track indexes from 115 index providers. S&P Dow Jones has $31.74 billion, the largest amount of ETF/ETP assets, tracking its benchmarks, which reflects that provider's 48.5% market share. FTSE is second with $15.39 billion and a 23.5% market share, followed by Barclays with $3.56 billion and a 5.5% market share.

The firm iShares, with $41.20 billion, is the largest ETF/ETP provider in Canada in terms of assets and has a 61.5% market share. BMO Global Asset Management is second with $14.97 billion and a 22.9% market share, and Mirae Horizons is third with $3.89 billion and a 5.9% market share. The top two ETF/ETP providers, out of nine, account for 84.3% of Canadian ETF and ETP assets, whereas the remaining seven providers each have less than a 6% market share.

ETFs listed in Canada have an asset-weighted average expense ratio of 0.38%. The cheapest products, at 0.33%, track fixed-income indexes; the most expensive are inverse ETFs at 1.15%. There are 8 ETFs with an expense ratio less than 0.1% and 66 ETFs with an expense ratio greater than 0.7%. At the end of September 2014, Vanguard's family of ETFs had an asset-weighted average expense ratio of 0.21%, making Vanguard the lowest-cost ETF provider in Canada.

Canada has some of the highest fees levied on mutual funds, and many advisers are paid to sell funds. The majority of advisers are licensed by the Mutual Fund Dealers Association (MFDA) and can sell only mutual funds; they are not allowed to buy and sell securities, which is what ETFs are typically considered to be. The minority of advisers are licensed by the Investment Industry Regulatory Organization of Canada and are set up to buy and sell individual stocks and ETFs. The ETF industry is working on developing a solution to allow MFDA advisers to sell ETFs.

The Canadian Securities Administrators, an umbrella group for Canada's 13 provincial and territorial securities regulators, has recently focused regulatory efforts on enhancing the transparency of fund fees for investors. Under Client Relationship Model 2, a regulatory action implemented in July 2014, new rules requiring more fee transparency were implemented.

The Canadian ETF industry hopes that as investors see and understand the fees that are paid to advisers for mutual funds and because most mutual funds do not consistently beat their benchmarks, financial advisers will be encouraged to use ETFs.

The ETF industry in Canada at the end of 2013 accounted for 6.3% of the overall Canadian mutual fund industry, which had 2,963 mutual funds with $941 billion in AUM.[37]

Latin America

The Latin American ETF industry had 43 primary listings of ETFs and 545 cross-listings, for a total of 588 listings, as of September 2014, as shown in **Figure A.3**. At that point, if we count only the assets for ETFs with their primary listings in Latin America, the region hosted $8.49 billion in assets from 20 providers listed on exchanges in, as **Table A.2** shows, Brazil, Chile, Colombia, and Mexico.

The majority of ETFs listed in Chile, Colombia, and Mexico are cross-listings of ETFs that have their primary listings in the United States or other markets. Pension funds in a number of Latin American countries have been allowed and encouraged to use foreign-domiciled ETFs to implement exposure to markets outside their home countries. Cross-listing an ETF makes it easier for pension funds to use the ETFs because the ETFs are listed and traded on the local exchange in the local currency like other securities.

Brazil is the biggest country in Latin America and has the largest asset management industry there, but it does not currently allow foreign ETFs to cross-list, and local pension funds are currently not allowed to invest in ETFs listed outside Brazil. In 2014, however, an ETF domiciled in Brazil

Figure A.3.   Latin American ETF Asset Growth, 2002–2014

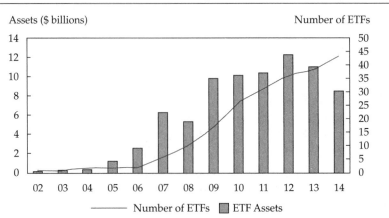

Number of ETFs   ETF Assets

Sources: ETFGI data sourced from ETF/ETP sponsors, exchanges, regulatory filings, Thomson Reuters Lipper, Bloomberg, publicly available sources, and data generated in-house.

---

[37]Investment Company Institute.

Table A.2.   Latin America: ETFs Listed by Country

Country	# of ETFs	# of Listings	Assets ($ millions)	ADV ($ millions)	NNA ($ millions)	YTD 2014 NNA ($ millions)	# of Providers	# of Exchanges
			September 2014					
Brazil	16	16	1,239	39	35	36	3	1
Chile	2	106	20	0	2	(5)	4	1
Colombia	3	18	1,582	8	14	47	4	1
Mexico	22	448	5,652	243	(130)	(2,697)	16	1
Total	43	588	8,494	291	(80)	(2,619)	20	4

Note: ADV = average daily volume; NNA = net new assets; YTD = year to date.
Sources: ETFGI data sourced from ETF/ETP sponsors, exchanges, regulatory filings, Thomson Reuters Lipper, Bloomberg, publicly available sources, and data generated in-house.

that holds a US-listed S&P 500 ETF as its only asset was allowed to list on the exchange.

The largest ETF provider in terms of assets is iShares, with $7.19 billion, reflecting an 84.6% market share; Itau Unibanco is second with $561 million and a 6.6% market share; BBVA Asset Management is third, with $364 billion and a 4.3% market share. The top 2 ETF providers, out of 20, account for 91.2% of Latin American ETF assets, and the remaining 18 providers each have less than a 5% market share.

The ETF industry in Latin America accounts for 0.9% of the Latin America mutual fund industry, which according to the Investment Company Institute (ICI), had 11,350 mutual funds with $1.20 trillion in AUM at the end of 2013.

Asia Pacific (ex Japan)

The Asia Pacific (ex Japan) ETF/ETP industry listed its first ETF, the Tracker Fund of Hong Kong (TraHK), in 1999. Based on AUM, the industry has been growing at a 30.6% annual rate over the past 10 years, as **Figure A.4** shows. Yet, it accounts for only 3.9% of global ETF and ETP assets. In September 2014, the industry had 557 ETFs and ETPs with their primary listings on an exchange in Asia Pacific (ex Japan) and 133 ETFs and ETPs with the majority cross-listed from domiciles outside the region, for a total of 690 listings with assets of $103 billion from 96 providers listed on 15 exchanges in 12 countries, as shown in Table A.1.

In Europe, a "passporting regime" exists for funds that comply with UCITS (Undertakings for Collective Investment in Transferable Securities)

Figure A.4. Asia Pacific (ex Japan) ETF and ETP Asset Growth, 2000–2014

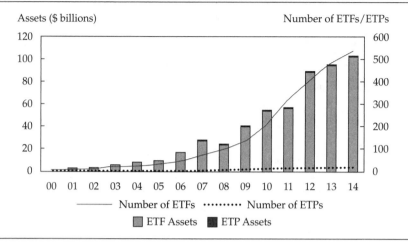

Sources: ETFGI data sourced from ETF/ETP sponsors, exchanges, regulatory filings, Thomson Reuters Lipper, Bloomberg, publicly available sources, and data generated in-house.

regulations. A passporting regime is an international agreement allowing funds domiciled in one country to be sold in other countries. The Asia Pacific region (ex Japan), however, does not currently have a fund passporting regime. Discussions are under way to create three different passporting regimes for the region.

The lack of a passporting regime means that ETFs that are locally domiciled and listed in one country cannot be registered for sale or cross-listed onto other exchanges in the region. The result is significant fragmentation and difficulty for ETFs and managers to benefit from economies of scale.

Most of the ETFs provide exposure to the local markets or the region. Some 86% of the assets are invested in the 417 equity ETFs and ETPs. The 51 fixed-income ETFs and ETPs account for 8.9% of the assets, and the 61 commodity products account for 2.1%. Five active ETFs in the region have 0.3% of the overall assets.

China A-share ETFs have been popular and actively traded because they provide an easy way to obtain exposure to mainland China without having to obtain a Qualified Foreign Institutional Investor quota. The original A-share ETFs listed in Hong Kong had to use derivatives called "p-notes." In the past two years, the RMB (renminbi) Qualified Foreign Institutional Investor scheme has allowed physical A-share ETFs to be listed in Hong Kong as well as in the United States and Europe.

Hong Kong has been a popular place to domicile and list ETFs. The hope is that the products will be allowed to be marketed in mainland China when the "mutual recognition" scheme between Hong Kong and China is introduced.

Hong Kong is seen as an institutional market, whereas Singapore is considered more a home of private banks and family offices. Hong Kong regulations have been more restrictive than some of the other Asian markets in terms of the types of ETFs that have been approved for listing. For example, Hong Kong has no leverage or inverse ETFs. In South Korea, however, many leverage and inverse ETFs have been listed and they are actively traded.

Singapore is considered to be faster to list products, but the increase over the past few years in regulations and requirements as to who can sell and who can buy ETFs has been associated with a significant decline in trading volumes in ETFs listed on the Singapore exchange.

Of the various stock exchanges in the region, trading volumes were highest on the Hong Kong Stock Exchange during September 2014. The $706 million in average daily turnover from ETFs and ETPs represents 31.4% of all ETF and ETP turnover in the Asia Pacific (ex Japan) region. In second place as of September 2014 was the Korea Stock Exchange with $652 million in average daily turnover and a 29.0% market share, followed by the Shanghai Stock Exchange with $559 million turnover and a 24.9% market share.

The largest ETF/ETP provider is iShares in terms of assets—$14.73 billion reflecting a 14.3% market share. SPDR ETFs are second with $13.88 billion and a 13.5% market share, followed by Samsung AM with $8.92 billion and a 8.7% market share. The top three ETF/ETP providers, out of 96, account for 36.4% of Asia Pacific (ex Japan) ETF/ETP assets, and the remaining 93 providers have less than a 9% market share each.

ETFs and ETPs in Asia Pacific (ex Japan) are tracking indexes from 121 index providers. China Securities Index (CSI) has the largest amount of ETF/ETP assets tracking its benchmarks—$27 billion, reflecting a 25.8% market share. FTSE is second with $20 billion and a 19.6% market share, followed by the Hang Seng Index with $15 billion and a 14.8% market share.

Only 3.6%, or 20 ETFs and ETPs, have gathered more than $1 billion in assets in the Asia Pacific (ex Japan) region, and these funds hold a combined total of $66 billion, or 67.2%, of the area's ETF/ETP assets. Fewer than one-fifth of funds in the region have more than $100 million in assets, which is typically regarded as the breakeven level for an ETF.

ETFs listed in Asia Pacific (ex Japan) have an asset-weighted average expense ratio of 0.55%. The cheapest products, at 0.2%, track fixed-income indexes; the most expensive are commodity ETFs, at 0.99%. Three ETFs have an expense ratio less than 0.1%, and 38 ETFs have an expense ratio greater than 1%.

Australia is the only market in the region that bans the payment of commissions to financial advisers for selling financial products. Australia has experienced an increase in the use of ETFs by financial advisers that are paid fees for advice as well as an increase in use by individual purchasers. In the rest of the region, financial advisers typically prefer to use funds and other products that they are paid to sell.

The ETF industry in Asia Pacific (ex Japan) accounted for 3.7% of the region's mutual fund industry, which, according to the ICI, had 13,453 mutual funds with $2.6 trillion in AUM at the end of 2013.

Japan

The Japanese ETF/ETP industry had 140 ETFs and ETPs with 182 listings and with assets of $89 billion from 18 providers listed on three exchanges at the end of September 2014. **Figure A.5** shows that the Japanese ETF/ETP industry has been growing at a 10.8% annual rate in the past 10 years. This rate is much lower than the 27.1% global ETF/ETP growth rate. Japan accounts for only 3.4% of global ETF and ETP assets.

Some 97% of the ETF/ETP assets are invested in products that provide exposure to equity benchmarks. Of the primary listings, only 2 are fixed-income, 11 are commodity, and 104 are equity ETFs or ETPs. Japan does have some leverage, inverse, and leverage/inverse products.

Figure A.5.   Japanese ETF and ETP Asset Growth, 2000–2014

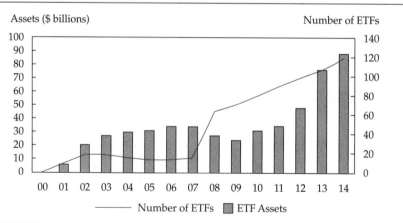

Sources: ETFGI data sourced from ETF/ETP sponsors, exchanges, regulatory filings, Thomson Reuters Lipper, Bloomberg, publicly available sources, and data generated in-house.

Japanese households have the majority of their estimated ¥1,500 trillion in assets invested in bank cash deposits. The Nippon Individual Savings Account, a tax-free savings program launched in January 2014, is expected to encourage investment in stocks, bonds, and other securities, including ETFs.

"ETF-JDRs," where JDR stands for Japanese Depositary Receipts, have been developed as a way to provide foreign ETFs in a structure that trades and settles like a Japanese security. Investors in ETF-JDRs are not required to open a foreign securities account and can use margin trading orders, which is the way the majority of retail investors trade.

The largest ETF/ETP provider in Japan in terms of assets is Nomura Asset Management with $41 billion, reflecting a 45.9% market share. Daiwa is second with $19 billion and a 21.7% market share, followed by Nikko Asset Management with $19 billion and a 20.8% market share. The top 3 ETF/ETP providers, out of 18, account for 88.3% of Japanese ETF and ETP assets; the remaining 15 providers each have less than a 9% market share.

Nikkei Indexes have the largest amount of ETF/ETP assets tracking its benchmarks—$46.5 billion, reflecting a 52.1% market share. The Tokyo Stock Exchange is second with $40.7 billion and a 45.6% market share. Third is S&P Dow Jones with $451 million and a 0.5% market share.

Nine, or 6%, of the 140 ETFs and ETPs have greater than $1 billion in assets. These funds and products account for a combined total of $80 billion, or 90.1%, of Japanese ETF/ETP assets. Twenty-eight, or 20%, have more than $100 million in assets, and forty-two have more than $50 million in assets.

ETFs listed in Japan have an asset-weighted average expense ratio of 0.21%. The cheapest products, at 0.18%, track equity indexes, whereas the most expensive are leveraged ETFs at 0.79%. Three ETFs have an expense ratio less than 0.1%, and 60 ETFs have an expense ratio greater than 0.3%.

According to the ICI, the ETF industry in Japan accounted for 9.9% of the Japanese mutual fund industry at the end of 2013, which had 4,922 mutual funds with $774 billion in AUM.

Europe

Nearly 15 years ago, in April 2000, the first ETFs were listed in Europe: The LDRs DJ STOXX 50 and the LDRs DJ Euro STOXX 50 were listed on the Deutsche Boerse, sponsored by Merrill Lynch International and acquired by iShares in September 2003. In the early years of the ETF industry, growth was faster in Europe than in the United States in terms of assets, number of products, and providers.

As **Figure A.6** shows, at the end of September 2014, the European ETF industry had 1,441 ETFs with 4,989 listings and assets of $433 billion, from

Figure A.6.   European ETF and ETP asset growth, 2000–2014

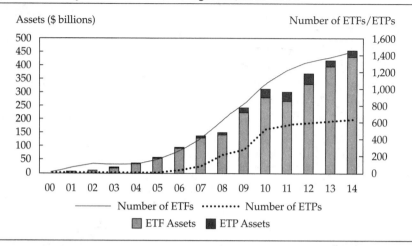

Sources: ETFGI data sourced from ETF/ETP sponsors, exchanges, regulatory filings, Thomson Reuters Lipper, Bloomberg, publicly available sources, and data generated in-house.

46 providers on 25 exchanges. As of the same date, the industry had 2,081 ETFs and ETPs combined with 6,233 listings and assets of $456 billion, from 51 providers on 26 exchanges.

In Europe, ETFs are structured as UCITS funds with at least one unit or share class traded throughout the day on at least one regulated market or multilateral trading facility with at least one market maker. The market maker takes actions to ensure that the value of shares of the ETF does not significantly vary from its net asset value and, where applicable, its indicative NAV.

The differences between the ETF/ETP industry in the United States and in Europe are numerous and substantial. The United States is one large homogeneous market, whereas Europe is fragmented because of multiple exchanges, tax and regulatory regimes (each jurisdiction can modify the EU guidelines for UCITS), languages, and currencies; home country bias; and captive and tied distribution models.

Registered investment advisers and retail investors account for 40%–45% of ETF assets in the United States but only 10%–15% in Europe. Independent financial advisers in the United Kingdom are increasing their use of ETFs because of the banning of payment of commission under the Retail Distribution Review (RDR), a legislative act implemented in the

United Kingdom in January 2013.[38] The Dutch RDR, which also bans the payment of commissions, was implemented in January 2014.

The providers of ETFs and ETPs in Europe have adopted a coffee shop approach to their offerings; that is, most firms offer similar products based on the same benchmarks. This situation is in contrast to the practice in the United States, where only one or two (and, rarely, three or more) ETFs are based on the same benchmark.

Of the top five indexes ranked by ETF/ETP assets in Europe as of September 2014, 22 ETFs/ETPs (with assets of $36.3 billion) were benchmarked to the S&P 500 Index; 35 ($28.5 billion) to Euro STOXX 50; 21 ($25.1 billion) to the DAX; 14 ($17.8 billion) to the MSCI World; and 16 ($16.1 billion) to the MSCI Emerging Market Index.

Equity products dominated: 898 equity ETFs and ETPs held $308 billion, or 67.6% of the assets; 304 fixed-income products held $92 billion, or 20.3% of the assets; 476 commodity products accounted for 8.8% of the assets, and 20 active products held $5.8 billion, or 1.3% of the assets. Alternative, currency, mixed, leverage, inverse, and leverage/inverse categories each account for less than 1% of overall assets.

In 2005, the move to UCITS III was significant because it allowed increased flexibility in terms of holdings within and across funds and also in the use of derivatives. Specifically, the regulation allowed more investment into ETFs that are UCITS. Prior to UCITS III, a UCITS fund could invest only 5% of its assets at most in other UCITS funds. Under UCITS III guidelines, a fund can invest up to 20% of its assets in another UCITS fund as long as its investment does not account for more than 25% of the NAV of the fund it is investing in.

UCITS III also allowed, for the first time, the use of listed and OTC derivatives as part of a fund's basic investment strategy, rather than simply for equitizing cash. This regulatory change in 2005 triggered the trend toward creating swap-based ETFs.

Many of the major brokerage firms/banks decided to become providers of ETFs through the swap structure as opposed to a security or physical ETF structure. Two models for swap-based ETFs have developed: The first uses one bank as a swap counterparty; the second uses swaps from multiple banks or has multiple swap counterparties.

UCITS III led to a blurring of the roles of the firms in the original ETF ecosystem. In the United States, asset managers are managers of ETFs. They work with banks and brokers that trade and distribute ETFs. In Europe, banks and brokers often both manufacture ETFs and trade and distribute

---

[38]For more information, see http://www.fsa.gov.uk/rdr.

them. Thus, they are often both a competitor to other ETF providers and a partner (as market makers) to those providers. This competitor/partner dilemma does not exist in the United States, where regulations do not allow asset managers and banks/brokerage firms to trade with affiliated entities.

In the United States, ETFs invest predominantly in a basket of physical securities or are physically backed with securities (except in the case of leveraged and inverse ETFs, where swaps and other derivatives are used). In Europe, the feuding over physical versus synthetic among providers has created uncertainty for investors trying to determine if, when, and what type of ETF they should consider. Because most ETFs in Europe are UCITS funds, it has also created a quandary for regulators. Although the number of synthetic ETFs in Europe has grown a great deal, the net new asset flows have primarily been in the physical ETFs, as is true for AUM.

In the past few years, some bank/brokerage firm ETF providers (such as Credit Suisse, Deutsche Bank, and Lyxor/Societe Generale) that historically focused on offering synthetic ETFs have moved their ETF business into their asset management operations and have begun offering physical ETFs. And they have converted some of their synthetic ETFs into physical. **Figure A.7** shows that, although the majority of ETF assets ($310.7 billion) in Europe are in products using physical replication methods, in terms of the number of ETFs, the majority (747 ETFs) use synthetic replication.

The explanations for these changes are that investors have shown a preference for physically backed ETFs when practical because such ETFs are easier to understand or less complicated than synthetic ETFs. Investors may also regard physically backed ETFs as less risky because the products minimize counterparty risk.

Many investors in Europe perceive ETFs listed in Europe as not being very liquid. They are confusing secondary trading with the true or primary liquidity of the underlying securities provided by the creation/redemption process. Secondary trading seems low because trade reporting for ETFs is currently not required in Europe under the Markets in Financial Instruments Directive (MiFID). It is estimated that about only one-third of trades in Europe are reported. With ETFs listed on 25 exchanges across Europe, volume is fragmented. Currently, no consolidated tape shows the total volume traded across the exchanges. MiFID II, which is planned to be implemented in 2017, is expected to require ETF trade reporting, and there will be a consolidated tape.

The firm iShares is the largest ETF/ETP provider in terms of assets—$210 billion, reflecting a 46.0% market share; db-X ETC is second with $54 billion and a 11.9% market share, followed by Lyxor Asset

Figure A.7. European Physical vs. Synthetic ETF Replication, 2005–2014

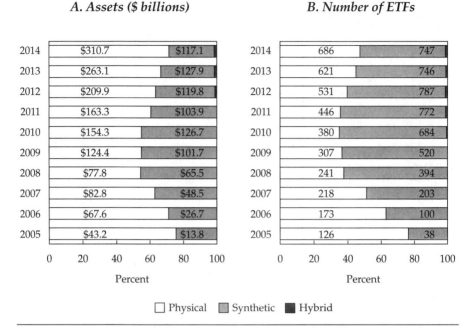

A. Assets ($ billions)   *B. Number of ETFs*

☐ Physical   ▨ Synthetic   ■ Hybrid

Sources: ETFGI data sourced from ETF/ETP sponsors, exchanges, regulatory filings, Thomson Reuters Lipper, Bloomberg, publicly available sources, and data generated in-house.

Management with $48 billion and a 10.5% market share. The top three ETF/ETP providers, out of 51, account for 68.4% of European ETF/ETP assets, whereas the remaining 48 providers each have less than a 5% market share.

There are 100 ETFs and ETPs in Europe with more than $1 billion in assets, and these funds and products hold a combined total of $261 billion, or 57.3%, of European ETF and ETP assets. About 30%, or 615, have gathered more than $100 million in assets, and 40%, or 817, have more than $50 million in assets.

ETFs listed in Europe have an asset-weighted average expense ratio of 0.35%. The cheapest products, at 0.23%, track fixed-income indexes; the most expensive are alternative ETFs at 0.77%. There are 15 ETFs with an expense ratio less than 0.1% and 48 ETFs with an expense ratio greater than 0.8%.

The ETF industry in Europe accounted for 4.2% of the European mutual fund industry at the end of 2013, which, according to the ICI, had 34,743 mutual funds with $9.4 trillion in AUM.

Middle East and Africa

At the end of September 2014, as **Figure A.8** indicates, the Middle East and Africa ETF industry had 46 ETFs with 56 listings and assets of $6 billion from 11 providers on eight exchanges. On that same date, the region's ETF and ETP industry had 675 combined ETFs and ETPs with 686 listings and assets of $41 billion from 21 providers listed on nine exchanges in nine countries.

The ETF industry in the Middle East and Africa region accounted for 3.8% of the mutual fund industry in the region, which according to the ICI, had 1,062 mutual funds with $143 billion in AUM at the end of 2013.

Table A.3 shows ETF/ETP data by country in the Middle East and Africa region. Counting only the assets for ETFs with their primary listing in the Middle East and Africa, $41.2 billion in assets from 21 providers was listed on exchanges in Israel, Nigeria, Saudi Arabia, South Africa, and the United Arab Emirates at the end of September 2014. Botswana, Ghana, Mauritius, and Namibia have had a few products cross-listed onto their exchanges from South Africa.

Figure A.8. Middle East and African ETF and ETP Asset Growth, 2000–2014

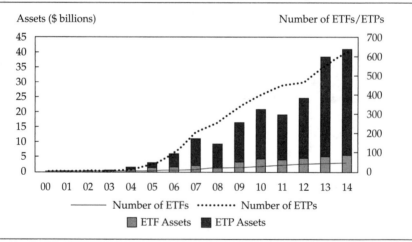

Sources: ETFGI data sourced from ETF/ETP sponsors, exchanges, regulatory filings, Thomson Reuters Lipper, Bloomberg, publicly available sources, and data generated in-house.

Table A.3. Middle East and Africa: ETFs and ETPs by Country

Country	# of ETFs	# of Listings	September 2014 Assets ($ millions)	ADV ($ millions)	NNA ($ millions)	YTD 2014 NNA ($ millions)	# of Providers	# of Exchanges
Botswana	—	3	—	0	—	—	2	1
Ghana	—	1	—	0	—	—	1	1
Israel	600	600	34,230	127	25	2,184	5	1
Mauritius	—	2	—	0	—	—	1	1
Namibia	—	4	—	2	—	—	2	1
Nigeria	1	2	17	0	—	—	2	1
Saudi Arabia	3	3	20	0	—	—	2	1
South Africa	70	70	6,936	14	—	—	12	1
United Arab Emirates	1	1	35	0	—	—	1	1
Total	675	686	41,238	143	25	2,184	21	9

Sources: ETFGI data sourced from ETF/ETP sponsors, exchanges, regulatory filings, Thomson Reuters Lipper, Bloomberg, publicly available sources, and data generated in-house.

Israel. At the end of September 2014, the Israeli ETF/ETP industry had 600 ETFs/ETPs and assets of $34 billion from five providers on one exchange. In Israel, all products domiciled and listed are currently ETNs, which are allowed under local regulations.

Tachlit Investment House, a wholly owned subsidiary of Israel Discount Bank Ltd, with $9.8 billion, reflecting a 28.8% market share, is the largest provider in terms of assets; KSM is second with $9.7 billion and a 28.3% market share, followed by Psagot Investment House with $7.3 billion and a 21.4% market share. The top two providers, out of five, account for 57.1% of Israeli ETN assets; the remaining three providers each have less than a 22% market share.

South Africa. Local ETFs have existed in South Africa for nearly 14 years. The Satrix 40 ETF, which is designed to track the FTSE/JSE (Johannesburg Stock Exchange) Top 40 index, was the first ETF to be listed on the JSE, which occurred in November 2000. Satrix was originally jointly owned by Sanlam and Deutsche Bank, but in August 2012, it became a wholly owned subsidiary of the Sanlam Group.

At the end of September 2014, the South African ETF industry had 41 ETFs with assets of $6 billion from seven providers listed on one exchange. As of that same date, the South African ETF/ETP industry had 70 ETFs and ETPs combined with assets of $7 billion from 12 providers listed on one exchange.

The growing middle class throughout Africa is drawing the attention of international investment organizations. The African Development Bank estimates that Africa's middle class will be bigger than China's by 2035. The workforce is younger than in many other regions of the world. Africa is a continent of 54 countries, which are very diverse from economic, cultural, language, and ethnic perspectives. By most measures, South Africa is Africa's leading economy.

South Africa is seen as an attractive financial market. With $236 billion in pension assets, it has the 10th-largest pension market in the world.[39] The Financial Services Board (FSB) has recently issued an RDR consultation. It is expected to follow the United Kingdom, Australia, and the Netherlands in implementing similar RDR reforms.[40]

Until recently, most foreign ETFs or mutual funds could not be registered for sale in South Africa because the local ETF/mutual fund or Collective Investment Scheme (CIS) rules require a structure where a trustee provides fiduciary control, acts as the custodian, and must be independent of the fund manager; a management company provides fund administration and marketing and usually outsources the investment decisions to an external asset management company.[41] This structure is not typical of funds and ETFs outside South Africa.

The FSB issued new regulations for foreign CIS that came into effect in early 2014. The new conditions rely on the acceptability of the home jurisdiction's regulations to the FSB rather than the structure of the scheme. The home regulator must have supervision and enforcement powers, and the ETF or fund must be available to retail investors.

The FSB's notice states, "The registrar is not adverse to UCITS compliant schemes as these schemes are intended for investment by retail investors." The registrar is, however, wary of permitting UCITS schemes that it deems to be riskier than the traditional plain-vanilla investments available in South

---

[39]This information is from Towers Watson, using data as of the end of 2013.

[40]See https://www.fsb.co.za/feedback/Documents/FSB%20Retail%20Distribution%20 Review%202014.pdf.

[41]A CIS is a type of investment vehicle used to pool investors' money. Through a CIS, investors can spread their investments in various asset classes, such as shares, bonds, and money market instruments. Investors share the risks and benefits of their investment in a scheme in proportion to their participatory interests in the scheme.

Africa. Accordingly, the registrar prefers UCITS ETFs and funds in which (1) derivatives are not used to leverage the portfolio and are covered at all times and (2) investment in synthetic instruments is not permitted.

Currently, no foreign ETFs are cross-listed on the JSE. The regulatory changes mean, however, that we will probably see foreign ETFs registered for sale and maybe even cross-listed in South Africa in the future. The ETNs that are listed on the JSE are regulated by the JSE, not the FSB, because they are seen as senior unsubordinated debt, not funds.

South African investors face limitations on where and how much they can invest because of foreign exchange controls and foreign investment limits. Pension funds and institutional investors must comply with Regulation 28, which stipulates a 20% limit on foreign assets. This percentage can be increased to 25% for exposure to other African countries. Retail investors have a foreign allowance of 4 million rand. Some local ETFs providing exposure to international benchmarks can be used by noninstitutional investors to diversify their investment portfolios with no exchange control limits.

Absa Capital, with $3.4 billion, reflecting a 49.5% market share, is the largest ETF/ETP provider in terms of assets. Satrix is second with $1.2 billion and a 17.4% market share, followed by db-X trackers with $1.0 billion and a 14.5% market share.

The ETF industry in South Africa, according to the ICI, accounted for 3.7% of the overall mutual fund industry in South Africa, which had 1,062 mutual funds with $143 billion in AUM at the end of 2013.

ETFs from South Africa have been cross-listed in Namibia (four ETFs), Botswana (three), Ghana (one), Mauritius (two), and Nigeria, which has one cross-listing and one primary listing. The first ETF in Egypt is expected to be listed soon. Kenya has recently initiated a request for proposal for work on the development of regulations for ETFs.

We expect the global ETF/ETP industry, the investors, and the surrounding ecosystem to continue to grow, as measured by many metrics, to pass $3 trillion in AUM and, globally, soon to surpass the assets in the global hedge fund industry.[42]

---

[42]For more information on trends in the global ETF/ETP industry, see www.etfgi.com.

RESEARCH FOUNDATION
CONTRIBUTION FORM

☑ **Yes**, I want the Research Foundation to continue to fund innovative research that advances the investment management profession. Please accept my tax-deductible contribution at the following level:

Thought Leadership Circle................ US$1,000,000 or more
Named Endowment...................... US$100,000 to US$999,999
Research Fellow .... US$10,000 to US$99,999
Contributing Donor........................ US$1,000 to US$9,999
Friend .... Up to US$999

I would like to donate $ _____ .

☐ My check is enclosed (payable to the CFA Institute Research Foundation).
☐ I would like to donate appreciated securities (send me information).
☐ Please charge my donation to my credit card.
　　　　　　■ VISA　■ MC　■ Amex　■ Diners

Card Number

___/___

Expiration Date　　　　　　　　Name on card　PLEASE PRINT

☐ Corporate Card
☐ Personal Card

Signature

☐ This is a pledge. Please bill me for my donation of $ _____
☐ I would like recognition of my donation to be:
　　■ Individual donation　■ Corporate donation　■ Different individual

PLEASE PRINT NAME OR COMPANY NAME AS YOU WOULD LIKE IT TO APPEAR

PLEASE PRINT　☐ Mr.☐ Mrs.☐ Ms.　　MEMBER NUMBER_____

Last Name (Family Name)　　　　　　First　　　　　Middle Initial

Title

Address

City　　　　　　　　State/Province　　　Country ZIP/Postal Code

Please mail this completed form with your contribution to:
The CFA Institute Research Foundation • P.O. Box 2082
Charlottesville, VA 22902-2082 USA

For more on the CFA Institute Research Foundation, please visit www.cfainstitute.org/learning/foundation/Pages/index.aspx.